Self Publishing Success
With
Kindle & CreateSpace

By Daniel Marks

ISBN-13: 978-1500856984
ISBN-10: 1500856983
Self Publishing Success With Kindle & Createspace

Table of Contents

Kindle Matchbook...5

Introduction..6

My First Experience In the Self Publishing World.....................9

Self Publishing Lingo..14

Tools of the Trade..23

In the Beginning...26

A Home for Your Masterpiece...27

Getting Familiar With Open Office..28

Formatting For the Digital Realm...33

Let's Format This Thing..35

Proofreading For Free!...36

Formatting Your Title Page...47

Formatting Your Table of Contents......................................49

Formatting for the Digital Age Phase 2................................57

Formatting With Calibre...61

Getting A Professional Cover..72

Kindle Direct Publishing...75

KDP Select...76

Kindle Direct Publishing Description.....................................78

Kindle Direct Publishing Categories.....................................81

Kindle Direct Publishing Preview Options.............................86

Kindle Direct Publishing Pricing..88

Formatting For Print...90

Createspace..91

Creating A Print Ready PDF File..96

Title and Legal Page for Print..109

Table of Contents for Print..110

Formatting the Header and Footer for Print..........................114

Creating A Print Ready PDF File...120

The Finishing Touch...124

Createspace Cover Options..128

Createspace Cover Dimensions and Properties.....................130

Synopsis for Print..134

Setting Up Distribution With Createspace.....................................136
Setting Up Pricing Through Createspace.......................................138
Proofing Your Print Masterpiece...142
Linking Digital and Print Editions...144
Backing Up Everything..145
Thanks...147
Additional Resources...148

Kindle Matchbook

If you purchased this book from Amazon, I highly suggest getting the Kindle version as well. It will make it easier to use all of the HYPERLINKS placed throughout the book.

The book is currently enrolled in a special promotional program with Amazon called Kindle Matchbook. This gives you the opportunity to purchase the Kindle version for only 99 cents.

Introduction

There is something really incredible about pouring your heart and soul into your first masterpiece and seeing it published in multiple formats, across multiple vendors all over the freaking planet. It is a huge accomplishment and it is immensely satisfying. It doesn't matter if you write fiction, short stories, essays, children's books, jokes, how-to books or steamy romance novels; wink wink, honk honk. There are endless possibilities waiting for you in the awesome world of self publishing. Are you ready to stake your claim in the literary world and unleash your inner author?

You could very easily become the next best selling author. This is not some made up BS story. It is 100% factual and it is happening every single day. This is the reality of one of the most gratifying experiences in the entire world: Self publishing.

Yeah, I said it and I believe it to be 100% true. Creating a book from start to finish and holding either a print copy in your hand, or reading a digital copy on one of today's high tech devices is one of the most gratifying experiences on planet earth, but do you know what's even better than that? Getting your first sale.

Do you know what's even better than that? Getting your first five star review.

Do you know what's even better than that? Having a reader tell you how much they enjoyed your book and having them tell you how much your book has inspired them.

Do you know what's even better than that? Having a parent tell you how your book has created a spark in their child's mind and fueled a new desire to read more books. How your book made them laugh and put a smile on their face.

Excuse me while I wipe the tears from my keyboard. That one always gets me right here. (Points towards heart) My silly rhyming children's book entitled: <u>Do Monster's Wear Undies</u> has done that numerous times, and I can't accurately relate in words how incredible it makes me feel.

Do you know what's even better than that? Being able to quit your boring old day job and enjoying your days surrounded by the beauty of the mountains in Vail, Colorado or the turquoise blue waters of some far away exotic island while you arrange the words of your next masterpiece.

Do you know what's even better than that? Getting your first one star review. Wait a minute, what? How is a one star review a good thing? Criticism is not a bad thing. There may be some valid points in that one star review that can help you boost your reading audience.

Reviews, be them good or bad are excellent indicators of

how your hard work is influencing your readers. If your masterpiece compels a person to point out what they may consider to be a flaw, it's just constructive criticism. Use this constructive criticism to your advantage.

All of these things can happen to you. This is the reality of self publishing.

The days of submitting your masterpiece to publishers and fearing a rejection letter are long gone. You now hold the power of publishing at your fingertips. You control your publishing destiny. You have been chosen my fellow wordsmith. It is up to you to deliver your magnificent work of art into the hands of people all over the world. Let that sink in for just a minute.

My First Experience In the Self Publishing World

It was difficult to see through the hundreds of camera flashes as I exited my black limousine and lightly placed my right foot down on the red carpet. I had arrived at the star studded world premier of a Hollywood blockbuster based on a book by none other than yours truly.

Beautiful women in long flowing gowns stopped to pose for photos as the paparazzi fought tooth and nail to snap the perfect shot. Men in custom tailored suits handcrafted by Giorgio Armani himself strutted their stuff along the long flowing red carpet that led to the interior of the infamous El Capitan Theatre, and here was little old me: a self published author.

I would like to tell you that this was what happened with my first experience in the self publishing world, but sadly it is not. My first attempt was what the kids of today would exclaim as an "Epic Failure." They would also probably point and laugh at me as well. Ha ha!

Yes, it is true. I will gladly admit it. My first attempt was a failure. I knew little to nothing about the self publishing world at the time, and I chalked this experience up to one of life's valuable learning lessons.

With my head held low, I walked down the street of sorrow

and contempt. I had been defeated, but then something happened. I met a person who was already succeeding in the self publishing world. He had several best selling books under his belt and he was making a healthy passive income.

He looked over my first attempt and instantly pointed out glaring flaws in my title, the cover and synopsis. "Go back to the drawing board," he said. The content of the book is fine, but your title, cover and synopsis; they suck. Ouch! But you know what? He was right.

I spent a few days looking over other books in the same genre. I noticed how lacking my book title was. It did suck. I studied all of the successful books in the same genre and a pattern started to emerge.

I was inspired! I was eager to make the important changes my poor dying book needed for a healthy revival. I quickly changed my title, created a new cover, tweaked the synopsis and posted all the changes online. My new changes would be live within 24 hours. Ah the wonders of modern technology!

I had worked tirelessly on my day off and decided it was time for bed. I had to report to the old 9 to 5 bright and early the next morning! Oh joy.

Sleep came easy that night. My dreams were full of words and turning pages.

The next morning at work, I decided to take a look at my book. Maybe my changes were already live. Maybe the world was ready to accept my masterpiece with open arms.

My changes were in fact live, but there was something else that was a huge surprise. I sold seven copies of my revised book while I was sleeping. I was stunned. I was flabbergasted. Yeah I know, flabbergasted is such a stupid word, but look at it. It just looks funny. FLABBERGASTED.

Anyways, my revised book made money in my sleep. This was that pivotal, life changing moment for me. I made money while I was sleeping. A giant light bulb appeared above my head and an alarm was going off somewhere up there too. Time to rinse, wash and repeat. There was nothing to stop me from building a literal empire based on nothing more than words. It's crazy when you think of it like that, but words can be powerful. They can be invigorating. They can be liberating!

This was around eight years ago. Today I have written, illustrated and self published more than two dozen books that have become best sellers. I am very proud of my accomplishments, but they have not all been shining success stories.

I would love to say that all of my published works have been huge successes, but they have not. That is just the nature of the game, but and this is a huge but. I now control my own destiny.

I now make more money while I sleep than I ever did at my boring old day job. If I choose not to work for a day, guess what happens? My books still sell. I still have an income stream. Guess what happens if I have a cold and I stay in bed for a week? My wife gets really sick of me whining and complaining, but the income from my book sales continues to roll in! It is freaking fantastic, but money is not the ultimate goal here. Sure it helps to buy the shiny things in life, but the ultimate goal is freedom. The freedom to do what you want with your life.

I am free! Ha ha ha! A little crazy with the power of freedom, but free to do whatever I want, whenever I want! At the time of this writing, I am traveling across the beautiful countryside of the United States in an RV with my entire family. I told you I was a little crazy. I can create my literary masterpieces from anywhere in the world, and I am happily doing it.

Don't take all of this the wrong way. I am not bragging, not in the slightest. I only mentioned these things for one simple reason. If I can do it, then so can you! In fact, I showed my 15 year old son how to do it. He wrote and self published his very first book and it became a bestseller, that little shit. But he did it! He took the initiative to create a bright and prosperous future for himself and so can you!

All right enough of this crap. Let's get your book published and into the hands of millions.

Self Publishing Lingo

Being an accomplished writer means you have a healthy vocabulary. You like playing with words. That's why you are here, but the self publishing world is full of strange new words, phrases or terms that you may have never heard of. I will be using some of these words throughout the rest of this epic masterpiece. I may have already done this. (sorry about that)

Before you dive headfirst into the waters of self publishing, it may be a good idea to look around a little. It can never hurt to familiarize yourself with more self publishing knowledge. Look before you leap they always say.

If you already consider yourself to be a self publishing linguistics major, then skip over this section, but if you think the term "bleed" has something to do with a paper cut that resulted from turning the pages of your shiny new proof, then you might want to keep reading. Knowledge is power they say.

First, let's take a look at file types. A good chunk of this book will revolve around publishing your masterpiece in the digital realm. Therefore, you need to have at least a small understanding of some of the different file types I am going to be throwing in your face.

MOBI

As of this writing, MOBI files are ebook files preferred by Amazon. This is the native file format for Kindle devices.

EPUB
Epub files are the industry standard file format for electronic publications, hence the name EPUB. I will show you how to properly format an EPUB for all vendors with a simple click of a button.

DOC
This is a basic word processing file brought to you by Microsoft. It most likely requires an expensive version of Microsoft's Office software to function. I will show you a free word processing software program that will read and write doc files.

PDF
PDF stands for pretty damn fancy. Okay not really. It stands for portable document file. This file type is an industry standard created by Adobe. PDF files can be read on a multitude of devices regardless of the installed operating system. It is a good, well rounded universal file.

I don't recommend PDF files for digital distribution through all of the major book vendors, but you will need a properly formatted PDF file when it comes time to get your book printed. Don't worry, I will show you how to do all of that too!

HTML

Hold on for this one. HTML stands for Hyper Text Markup Language. If you have ever viewed a raw HTML file, then you know it looks very much like a foreign language. This is the language that all web pages were originally written in. How's that for a nice little history lesson?

Learning HTML is beyond the scope of this book. There are already giant publications addressing this pretty easy to pick up computer language.

ODT

This is yet another word processing file type that we will be working with a little later using a great FREE piece of software called Open Office.

Those are all of the major document files related to the self publishing world. Give yourself a little pat on the back, you have gained powerful knowledge. Let's move on to image files.

JPG

These are the most common image files. Most digital cameras on today's market save pictures in this format. They are compressed, making them easier to send through cyberspace.

GIF

There is an ongoing Internet debate on how this file name is pronounced. Some say it is pronounced like JIF, others says it is pronounced like GIF. Who cares, right? Not all electronic ereader devices like the GIF file. I don't recommend using GIF files in any way shape or form.

PNG

The portable network graphics file or PNG is fairly common. PNG files can be a little on the large size. This can create a rather unfortunate problem if your book is image heavy. Larger files require more Internet bandwidth to send. Amazon charges you a delivery fee based on the size of your digital book. The larger your book is, the more it costs to deliver. Image heavy books should always use slightly compressed JPG files. They produce a smaller book file and more profit in your bank account. Whew!

Let's move away from pretty pictures and look at specific terms related to the books themselves.

Active TOC

Active TOC or active table of contents can only be found in digital books. It is an "active" table of contents that can be easily accessed at anytime. This makes it easier for a reader to navigate to the juicy parts of the book. Readers enjoy this feature.

Creating an active table of contents seems to elude quite a few people. I will show you how to format your masterpiece with a proper active table of contents.

Back Matter

This is the fat that grows on an author's back because they have spent too much time sitting at the computer. Of course, I'm not serious. Back matter is any content that lives in the last few pages of your book that is not directly related to the meat of your story. Things like: a simple thank you, request to leave a review, more best sellers by this author. You get the idea.

Barcode
The good old bar code will only be needed for a print copy of your masterpiece, and you don't even have to do anything to get it done.

Binding
Again, this term refers to books printed in the physical world. When we get to the section on getting your books printed, we will talk a little more about your binding obligations. Ha ha. Did you see what I did there? Binding obligations. That is my sad attempt at making a joke. Now you understand why none of my best selling books are comedic masterpieces.

Bleed, Bleeding or Bleeds
Yet another print only term. Have you ever wondered how book covers are always perfectly lined up and the fancy color printing goes all the way to the edge? Me neither, but I had to learn about this stuff when I was formatting my book for print.

Bleeds come into play for both the inside of your book and

the physical cover. Book covers always look perfect because the outside edge of the books bleeds over. The excess print or bleed is then cut.

Blurb

A small portion of your book that might entice a reader to purchase the entire book and help you on your quest for world domination! Muw ha ha ha!

CSS STYLES

If you are at the point in your self publishing career where you need to know what CSS styles are, then you have crossed the line. CSS styles were originally used to format web pages. They are now being used to format ebooks as well. You do not need to know anything about CSS styles to self publish your first few books, or any for that matter.

If you get into creating beautiful children's books, then you will need to learn more about CSS styles. This book will not cover that topic! Sorry, but I am trying to keep this book as simple as possible.

Ebook

This is your masterpiece in electronic format.

Front Matter

Remember back matter? This is the same exact thing, but in the front of your book. It may reside before the story and the table of contents.

Genre

A particular style of book. Science fiction is a genre. Romance is a genre. Potato chips are not. They are fatty, salty and bad for you. Stay away from them.

ISBN

At one point in time, someone came up with the great idea of applying a unique identifying number to every book published. That idea is the ISBN or International Standard Book Number. Sounds fancy doesn't it? You will need an ISBN for print books. I will cover that at the proper place and time.

Interior

This is the bulk of your masterpiece. This is everything under the cover. The whole enchilada. The whole shebang. The meat and potatoes. Your epic, life altering Pulitzer price winning masterpiece!

Mass Market Paperback

This is what the print version of your book will be. It is an industry standard paperback book where the cover is glued to the spine.

Niche

Pretty much the same as genre in this circumstance.

Print on Demand

Ahh, this is the beautiful method of having your masterpiece printed only when someone orders it. You do not have to pay any up front costs utilizing a print on demand method. The costs associated with printing your masterpiece come directly out of the sale. Yes, it costs more to print this way, but you have no out of pocket expenses. Once you are a New York Times best seller, then you can switch from the old faithful print on demand method.

Print Ready

This term refers to making sure your cover and the interior of your masterpiece are both formatted perfectly for print. They are "print ready."

Proof

This term can have a couple of meanings in the self publishing world. To "proof" your book means to remove any common spelling or grammatical errors from your masterpiece.

A "proof" copy of your book is the very first printed copy that you must look over with a fine toothed comb. Once you agree everything looks good, then your book is ready for the masses.

Your original proof can be filed away for later. Once you become a world famous author, you can sell that proof copy of your book on Ebay for a zillion bucks. That's what you call planning ahead!

Synopsis

The synopsis is the sales pitch of your masterpiece. It must lure in a hungry reader and make them want to buy. Creating a perfect synopsis is difficult. I suggest looking at other books similar to yours to get a good idea of how to craft the perfect synopsis. You have to tease the reader without giving away any major plot points.

Trim Size
This is the final size of your book after it has been printed and any excess ink or paper has been cut away.

That's it. You have now filled your brain with common terms related to the self publishing world. Now you can talk with other budding writers and sound like a self publishing expert.

Tools of the Trade

You are going to need some additional tools if you want to get the most out of this insanely valuable self publishing guide. Don't ask questions at this moment. Just make sure you have these things. All will become clear in the not so distant future.

Coffee or Tea
Coffee or tea are both excellent stimulants that can help you keep your thoughts nice and clear during this process. I prefer tea. Coffee makes me completely crazy!

A Good Night's Rest
I find it really difficult to stop when writing, proofing, formatting or doing any sort of self publishing. I want to deliver my hard work into the hands of the masses, but overworking yourself can be counter productive. You should already know how important a good night's sleep is.

A Decent Computer
If you do not own a computer and loathe the idea of letting this wonderful piece of technology take part in your life, then stop right now. This book will be useless to you. It revolves heavily around computers. Heck, the entire self publishing world revolves heavily around computers. If you refuse to own a computer, then you will have to pay someone to do every step of the self publishing process for you. That kind of takes the "self" out of self publishing.

If you do already own a computer, then fanfreakingtastic! You are ready to rock and roll. If your computer of choice is a MAC, then you may also have a difficult time with this self publishing masterpiece. Everything I will be showing you about the self publishing process will involve using a PC. With that said, you can still use the vital information in this book and apply it to your MAC, just don't add cheese. Get it? MAC and cheese. Yeah, I did just go there and I feel like less of a human being for it. Sorry...

A Reliable Internet Connection
The world of self publishing will have you sending and uploading files all over cyberspace. You can't do this without a reliable Internet connection.

Do You Need A Super Computer?
For the self publishing novice, a basic computer is all that is required. You do not need a computer that operates at 2 million gigaflops with a quad core GPU, 5 terabytes of ram and a 16 terabyte hard drive. Overkill! A basic computer is fine.

Apache Open Office
This is a FREE office production suite packed with powerful features we will be using throughout this book. Download it now at the following link. It's free!

https://www.openoffice.org/

Calibre

This is a FREE powerful piece of ebook management software that will help you self publish your book in every conceivable format. It will be required for certain sections of this book. Download your free copy at the following link:

http://calibre-ebook.com/

If for any reason computer software intimidates you, don't let it. I will be holding your hand through every process where these pieces of software are being used. I will also openly offer my assistance if you feel scared, lost or confused. Seriously. I want you to succeed. If you have any questions email me: wordsaremything@gmail.com

I will be glad to help.

In the Beginning

If I could be sitting there right beside you at this moment, I would be reading the following paragraph using a sophisticated teacher's voice. Try it.

In today's class on creating a literary masterpiece, we will discuss the finer points of character development, plot twists, story arcs, hooks and classic landscape settings for modern literature. We will be painting a vivid picture with nothing but words and the canvas will be your intended reader's mind. Are there any questions?

Hey wait a minute. This is a book on self publishing on a budget, not creating a literary masterpiece. We will not be discussing the finer details of character development or any of that nonsense. I will not tell you how to write your book, but I will show you how to use FREE tools to format and self publish your masterpiece like a pro! Let's get started!

Hopefully you have already downloaded the two free tools I listed under the chapter titled: Tools of the Trade. If you haven't done this yet, then you need to right now because without these two great pieces of software, YOU SHALL NOT PASS!

A Home for Your Masterpiece

Throughout this book we will be working with computer files. If your computer organizing skills are a little lacking, then you may find it difficult to achieve world domination through self publishing.

The very first thing you need to do is create a space on your computer where you plan to store all the files associated with your masterpiece. You may have 1st drafts, 2nd drafts, proofed copies and cover files. All of these files should reside in one single location. Trust me on this. It will make things much easier on you in the long run.

A little later in this insanely cool book, I will be showing you how to move all of those files to the Cloud! Yeah, we are going to get high tech, but don't worry. It's really simple.

Go ahead and make that new home on your computer for all of your files. I will be waiting for you when you get back. While you're at it, order me a pizza will you?

Getting Familiar With Open Office

If you are already familiar with basic word processing functions in programs like Microsoft Word, then you can skip this chapter. This chapter is a basic introduction to the functions of Open Office. Let's dive in!

Go ahead and Open Open Office. That looks like a typo doesn't it? "Open Open Office." It's not. When Open Office starts, you will be presented with a fancy looking splash screen like the image below. Marvelous huh? Choose the Text Document option.

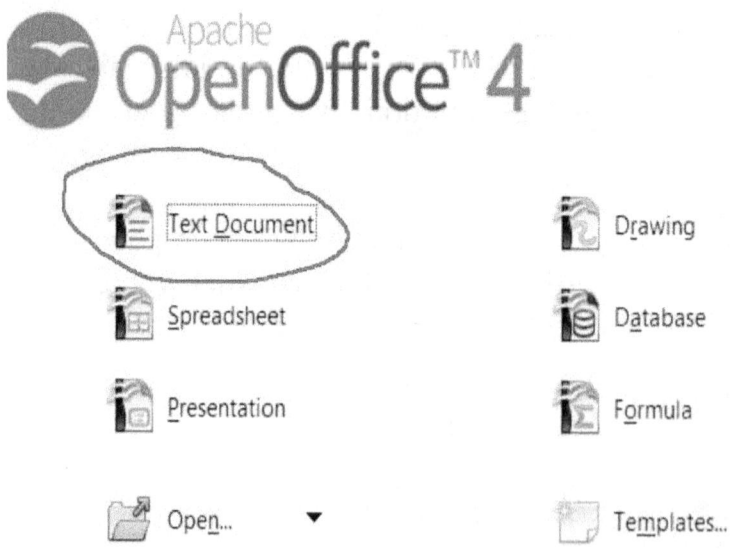

You should now see a blank text document with a single lonely blinking cursor. Look at the cursor. It's taunting you, isn't it? It wants you to type some text. Go ahead and type something. It doesn't matter what you type. It could be anything. Just give it a try.

This is how you use the word processing functions of Open Office. It's easy, huh? Now I will explain some of the basic toolbar functions along the top.

Look over the word based menu system.

File   Edit   View   Insert   Format   Table   Tools   Window   Help

Click each of these words and look over all the options each one gives you. There's a lot of stuff up there isn't there? Don't let that overwhelm you because we won't be using even a quarter of those functions up there.

Now let's look at the formatting bar. It will become your partner, the butter on your toast, the secret sauce!

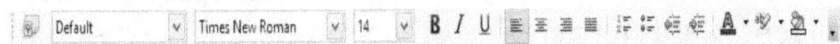

I will explain each function starting from the left to the right.

Hover your pointer over the first little icon on the left. A little text bubble should pop up that says "Styles and Formatting F11." Go ahead and click it. Your styles and formatting window should magically appear. The F11 key on your keyboard will do the same thing. Close it for now by clicking the red X in the upper right corner of the Styles and Formatting box.

The next little section that says "default" is your style selection menu. This allows you to change or apply different styles to different blocks of text. Go ahead and give it a try.

Type some text. Highlight the text by clicking behind the text, holding down your mouse button and dragging your pointer towards the left side of the screen. Your text should now be highlighted. Click the little drop down arrow and choose a style. Notice how your text is transformed? Whoa dude, that's outasite!

All of the text in your masterpiece, not including chapter titles, table of contents and front matter should use the "default" style.

The next selection box is your font selection menu. Highlight some text and choose a new font from this menu. Your text should change to this new font. I recommend using just one font throughout your entire masterpiece. I prefer Times New Roman.

The next selection box allows you to change the size of your text. Go ahead and try it. Don't use a font size over 14 for your books. Size 12 is optimal.

Next you will see a Bold "**B**", a crooked "*I*" and a "U" with an underline. The "**B**" will change your selected text to a **bold font**, the crooked "*I*" will *italicize* your selected text and the "U" will create an underline under your selected text.

The next four selections allow you to align your text. The far left selection will align your selected text to the left. The next choice will align your selected text in the center of your masterpiece. The next choice will align your selected text to the right. The final selection of the four will allow you to justify the selected text. This will evenly display one line of text across the entire width of the page.

Go ahead and play with these options. Get comfortable with them. They should smell like a comfortable old shoe. Feel, I mean they should FEEL like a comfortable old shoe.

All of the other options will not be necessary at this time. You don't need to know anything about margins, page gutters or any of that nonsense. Open Office will suit us perfectly with it's default settings.

Formatting For the Digital Realm

Just like life, the self publishing world is full of choices. Formatting being one of the biggest choices you will need to make. Here is the problem. Almost every vendor wants your masterpiece in a different format and that is just the digital end of things. When it comes time to turn your masterpiece into a paperback book, then you will need to create yet another format. Just trying to wrap your head around all of these different formatting options and procedures can quickly drain your brain.

I have already mentioned that I am a little crazy and a lot cheap, but I am also a control freak when it comes to my masterpiece. I want to be able to fine tune every aspect of my best seller. After all, this is my baby.

The combination of these three traits could be a good or a bad thing depending on how you look at things. I tend to see them as a good thing. The crazy trait gives me the ability to dive right in with a reckless disregard for possible mistakes. The cheap trait helps me locate as many FREE resources as possible, and the control freak in me does not want to be limited by another person or some silly piece of software.

It is because of these three traits that I have finally mastered formatting my books in the easiest, yet cheapest way possible and I am going to tell you exactly how I do it. This method works great for your basic book that is packed to the gills with pretty words.

If your masterpiece is full of bright colored images, you will need to dig much deeper. You will need to learn CSS styles and HTML code if you want your book to look perfect. I DO NOT COVER these techniques in this book. They would be considered advanced techniques that are beyond the scope of this book.

The complete free way takes more time, but costs you nothing. You will also pick up a wealth of knowledge from self publishing your book using the FREE methods.

Let's Format This Thing

Do you have a fresh pot of coffee brewing, or some refreshing tea? You might need it with the following chapters because we will be diving deep into two very different pieces of software. Both of which are FREE!

You will need to download a FREE copy of Apache Open Office. I already told you all about this in the chapter called: Tools of the Trade. If you skipped over it, then go back and read it. You will need Open Office when it comes time to format your masterpiece for print too.

We will also be using that other wonderful FREE piece of software I told you about called Calibre. It will be the last and final step towards creating a perfectly formatted book for the digital masses.

From this point on, I am doing something we are all never told to do. I will be *assuming* you have finished typing up your literary masterpiece. If it isn't done yet, then get back to work!

Give your masterpiece a once over and make sure everything looks good. Make sure font types and sizes are correct. If your masterpiece uses page numbers, remove them. They are not allowed in digital publications.

Proofreading For Free!

Dear reader, we interrupt this formatting lesson to bring you this urgent message on proofreading procedures.

I know I said we would start formatting your masterpiece, but I have to share this earth shattering nugget of wisdom with you.

Hiring a professional proofreader is always the best choice, but they can be pretty pricey. If you are a budding new writer, you most likely don't have that massive marketing train barreling down the tracks pushing your book sales to the top of all of the best selling lists. We are trying to keep this whole self publishing thing as cheap as possible.

Your first attempt at self publishing may very well be an epic failure like mine was. Seeing your hard work fail is tough. Having to finance and pay for your hard work is even tougher. Let's keep this cheap.

Once you become the next best selling author, then you will have the luxury of interviewing proofreaders. If you are famous enough, you may even be able to hire a famous Hollywood celebrity to personally read you your masterpiece. Who would you pick?

You worked hard on your masterpiece. Don't let little unseen errors make your work look less professional.

Proofreading For Free!

Readers will be quick to point out misspellings and bad grammar in a review. (Don't even think about doing that. I am pouring out my heart and soul to you here!)

Other readers may see this as bad and decide not to buy your book. Your book will then die a slow, miserable death and your career as a famous author gets erased from the archives. Poof, you're done.

Proofreading is essential, and being the crazy mixed up cheapskate that I am, I have discovered how to get all of my works proofread for free! Check out this insanity!

For my first round of proofreading, I always turn to my faithful and reliable sexy British female. She is always ready to read anything I throw her way, and the best part is the cost. She doesn't charge me a single penny! Free is your friend in the self publishing world, and I am a cheapskate. I have scoured the self publishing world for either FREE resources or resources that are dirt cheap. They are all yours for the taking.

Right now, at this very moment, I bet you would like to know more about my free British female proofreader, wouldn't you? Well today is your lucky day because I am going to show you exactly how you can use her services.

My sexy female British proofreader is my computer. By using a text to speech program, I can choose from a myriad of voices to easily read back my masterpiece. The end result is pretty freaking amazing and it is free! Here is what you need to do.

First you must have Google Chrome installed on your machine which is FREE. You can find Google Chrome here:

https://www.google.com/intl/en-US/chrome/browser/desktop/index.html

Once you have Google chrome installed, you will need to install the FREE Speak It text to speech extension. Don't worry, all you have to do is click a button. It's simple.

You can Google "Speak It Extension For Chrome," or you can download the extension here:

https://chrome.google.com/webstore/detail/speakit/pgeo lalilifpodheeocdmbhehgnkkbak?hl=en-US

You are almost ready to use your new personal proofreading assistant, but first you will need to setup a FREE Google account. You will need this later when we start talking about backing up your work. If you already have a FREE Google account, then you are one step ahead of the game. If you don't, get one now at the following link:

https://accounts.google.com/signup?service=mail

Now that you have all that out of the way, you can get to work proofreading your masterpiece. Open up Google Chrome and go to: drive.google.com

This is Google's FREE online storage and document creating software suite. Pretty sweet right? Pun intended. Now for the fun part.

Once you have signed in to your Google Drive account, you want to look for one magic red create button. It looks like this.

On my computer, this magical red button appears in the upper left corner. Move your cursor over this create button and click it. You should see something like this.

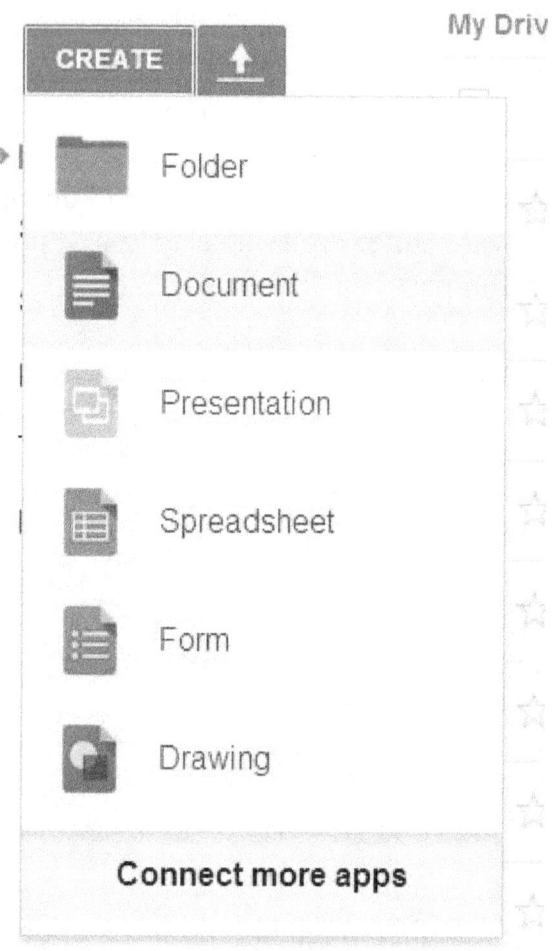

Click the blue document icon. You should be magically transported to Google's FREE word processing program. Don't be afraid of it. It is just like any other word processing program. You type and words appear. It's simple. Go ahead and type something really cool about yourself. Something like, "Your name goes here is the coolest person in the world."

Now it is time to access your proofreader. An American voice is selected by default. I will show you how to change it in a minute. First, you have to find the proofreader. For whatever reason, they did not make this thing very obvious. On my computer, the proofreader icon is tiny and it appears in the upper right corner like a speaker Icon. It looks like this.

Move your cursor over that little speaker icon and click it. If everything works as it should, your computer should be reading that super cool sentence you typed about yourself. You should also now see this.

The big button in the middle will pause your new proofreader and the little square in the upper left corner will stop her completely.

Now you just need to copy and paste your epic masterpiece into Google's free word processor. I recommend only copying and pasting small portions of your work at a time. If you don't know how the copy and paste functions work on a computer, here is a brief tutorial.

Open the software you used to type your epic masterpiece. Use your cursor to select a block of text. While the text is highlighted, hold down the "ctrl" key. While holding down the "ctrl" key, press the "c" key. This is the keyboard shortcut for the copy function. You could also move your cursor up to the word edit, click it and then click copy.

Your highlighted block of text is now copied to a virtual clipboard. Now you just need to paste it into Google's FREE word document. You should already have this open. This is where you typed that really cool sentence about yourself. Get rid of that sentence and place your cursor at the beginning of your blank document. Hold down the "ctrl" key. While holding down the "ctrl" key, press the "v" key. This is the keyboard shortcut for the paste function.

Your text should magically appear in the FREE Google word document. Click that little speaker button and let your new virtual proofreader get to work.

What? You don't like the FREE proofreading voice? No problem, let's change it. **Right click** that little speaker icon. You should see this.

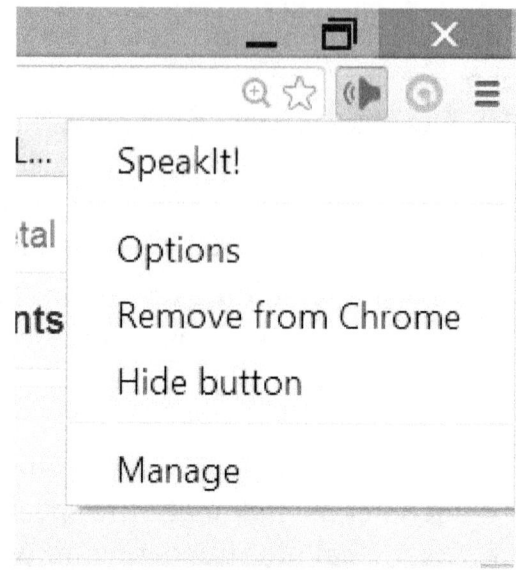

Click options and you should now see this.

Proofreading For Free!

Click the voice drop down menu and you should see this.

Proofreading For Free!

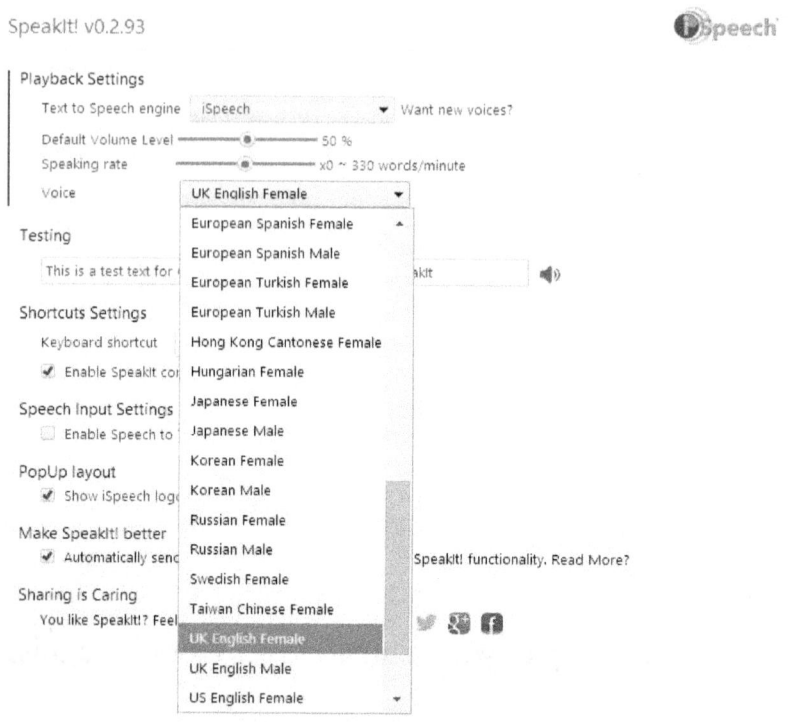

There you have it. Your very own personal proofreader available in a huge variety of voices, accents and languages. Go ahead and play around with this feature. It can be quite entertaining.

Once you are done here, have a family member proofread your masterpiece as well. More eyes will help you fine tune every word!

Formatting Your Title Page

You may now return to your regularly scheduled lesson on formatting for the digital age.

Formatting your title page is simple. Your title should be big and bold. Any font size over 18 should work just fine. Make sure the title is the "default" style not a "Heading" style.

Underneath the title, you may want to include your author name using a smaller font size. I prefer a size 12. It is generally a good idea to let people know who wrote this masterpiece. How are your fans going to stalk you in the wee hours of the morning if they don't know your name? A pen name might be a good idea, huh?

Under the author name you can put the legal mumbo jumbo in the same size font as the author name.

Then you may want to place the typical warning that copying your book is not allowed unless someone pays you a million bucks. I use the same font size for this, but I make it **BOLD**. Here is a sample title page screen shot for you.

Super Cool Pulitzer Price Winning Epic Masterpiece of Sauciness

By Mark Smith

Copyright 2014 and Beyond All Rights Reserved

No part of this book may be reproduced, copied, or transmitted in any form without the written consent of the author.

Format your title page accordingly and get ready to move on!

Formatting Your Table of Contents

The next big step requires formatting your Table of Contents. In order to do this we have to back the truck up for just a second. Your chapter titles will make up the bulk of your table of contents and if they are not formatted correctly, the table of contents will be a huge mess. Let's make sure the chapter titles are formatted correctly. Here is what needs to be done.

Your chapter titles must be formatted as Heading 1 tags. Highlight your chapter title and and use the style selection menu in the upper left corner.

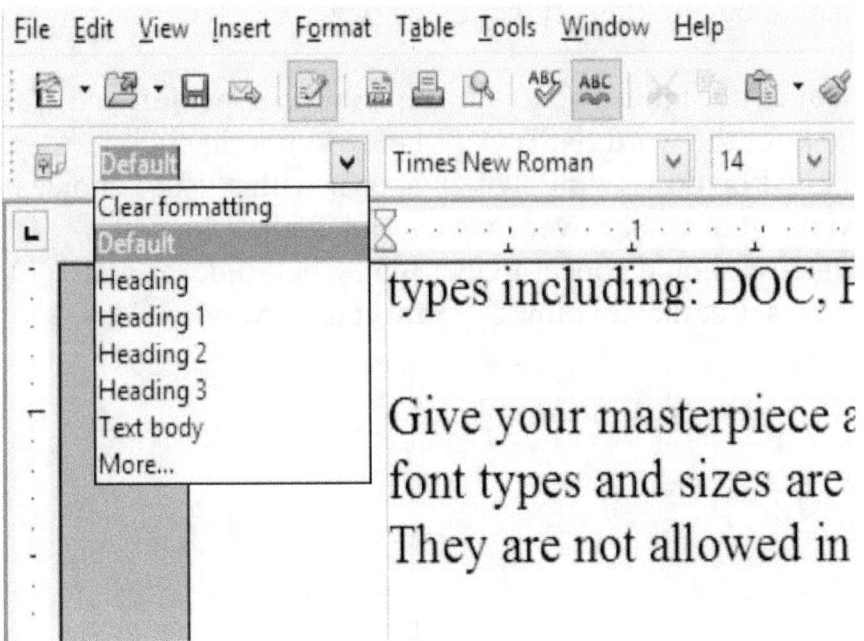

While your chapter title is still highlighted, choose Heading 1. Your chapter title should now be big and bold. Do this to the rest of your chapter titles and save your masterpiece. Now we need to create your table of contents. It is a simple process.

Go back to your title page. Underneath all of your credits, click your mouse once so that you have a blinking cursor underneath all the important stuff.

Hold down the "ctrl" key. While you are holding down the "ctrl" key press the "enter" key. This will create a new blank page for your table of contents. Your little cursor should be blinking on that blank page.

Move your mouse up to the menu in the upper left and look for the word INSERT. When you find it, click it. A large drop down window will appear with a list of choices. Move your cursor over Indexes and Tables. A small window should appear to the right. Click Indexes and Tables. Let the next image show you the way.

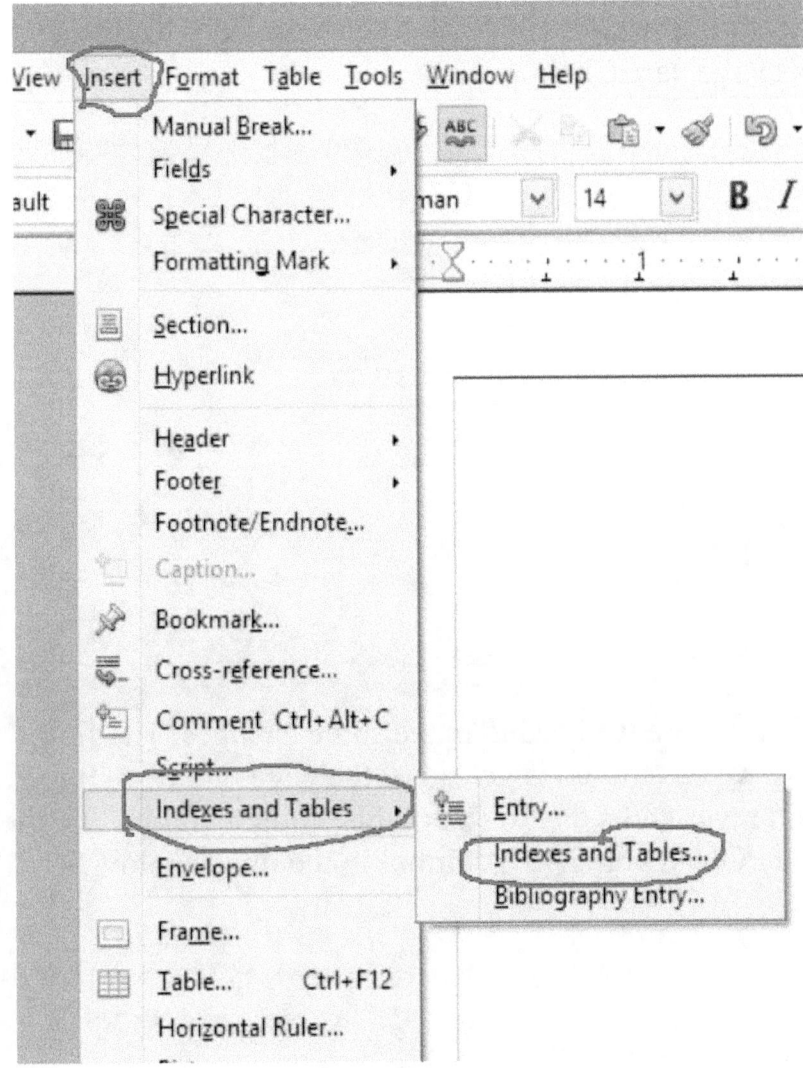

You will now be presented with your Table of Contents options like the image below.

Pay close attention to the tab I have circled. This is the ENTRIES tab. Click it.

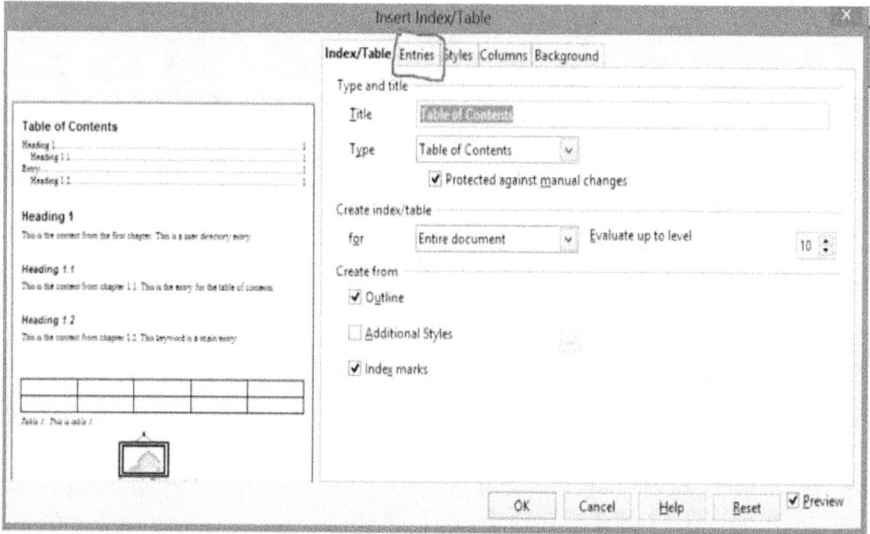

This is where we need to make some changes. The first thing we have to do is get rid of the page numbers. It took me forever and a day to figure this stupid part out. See the little POUND or HASH symbol in the image below?

Formatting Your Table of Contents

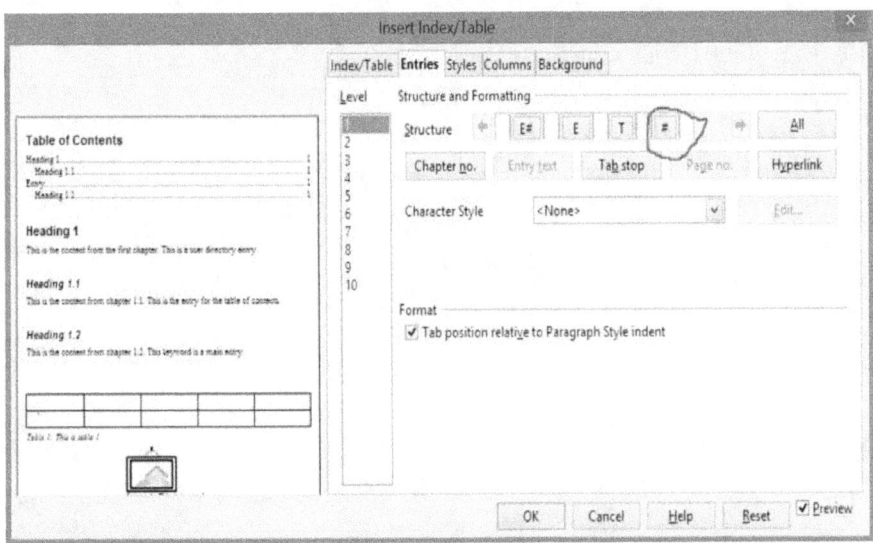

Click that little POUND or HASH symbol and then press the DELETE key on your keyboard. The POUND or HASH symbol should disappear. The page numbers are now gone!

Now we have to make our current table of contents clickable links. Here's what you do. In the same area where you removed the POUND or HASH symbol, you need to click in that little tiny blank spot behind the T and then click the button that says HYPERLINK. Check out the image below.

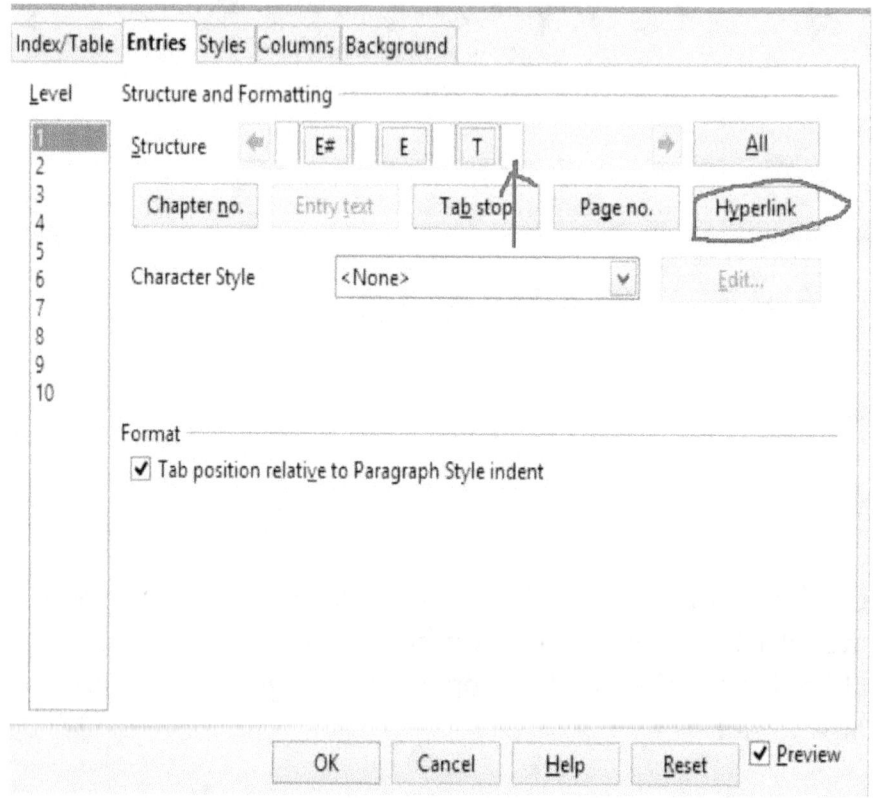

An LS should now magically appear.

Now you need to do the same exact thing before the E#. When you do this another LS appears and the first LS changes to an LE. LS stands for Link start and LE stands for Link End. You should now have something like the image below.

Formatting Your Table of Contents

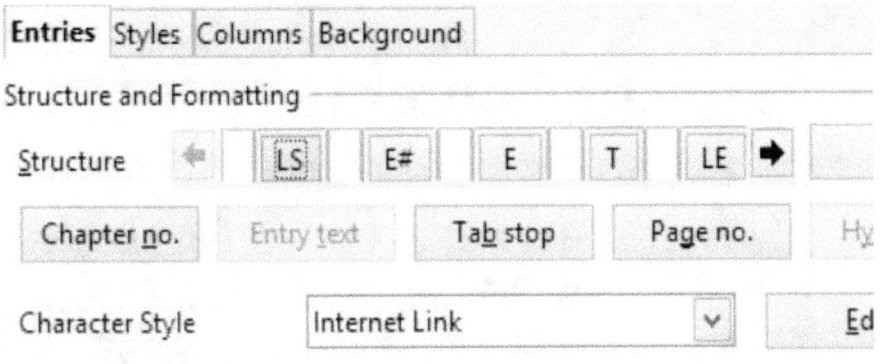

One final step, and your Table of contents will be all done. Click the OK button

You should now see a perfectly created table of contents in your masterpiece. Save your masterpiece and move on to the next step.

If you make any changes to your masterpiece that would alter the accuracy of your Table of Contents, you will need to update it. To do this, simply RIGHT CLICK anywhere in your current Table of Contents and click Update Index/Table. Here is an image example.

Table of Contents

Introd~~uction~~
My F
Self F
Tools
In the
Gettin
Form
Let's
Proof
Form
Form

Style	▶	Publishin
Alignment	▶	
Line Spacing	▶	
Case/Characters	▶	
Update Index/Table		
Edit Index/Table		
Delete Index/Table		
Edit Paragraph Style...		

Formatting for the Digital Age Phase 2

It's all down hill from here. Your masterpiece is almost ready for the digital masses. You have done some of the most difficult tasks you will do in this epic instruction guide. Give yourself a pat on the back. You deserve it.

For the first part of this section, we will still be working with your masterpiece in Open Office. If you closed it, you need to open it again.

We are going to magically transform your masterpiece into an HTML document. This is some heavy stuff. Are you ready? Of course you are. Let's go.

Move your cursor up to the word FILE in the menu in the upper left. Click it and then click the SAVE AS command. Here is an image example.

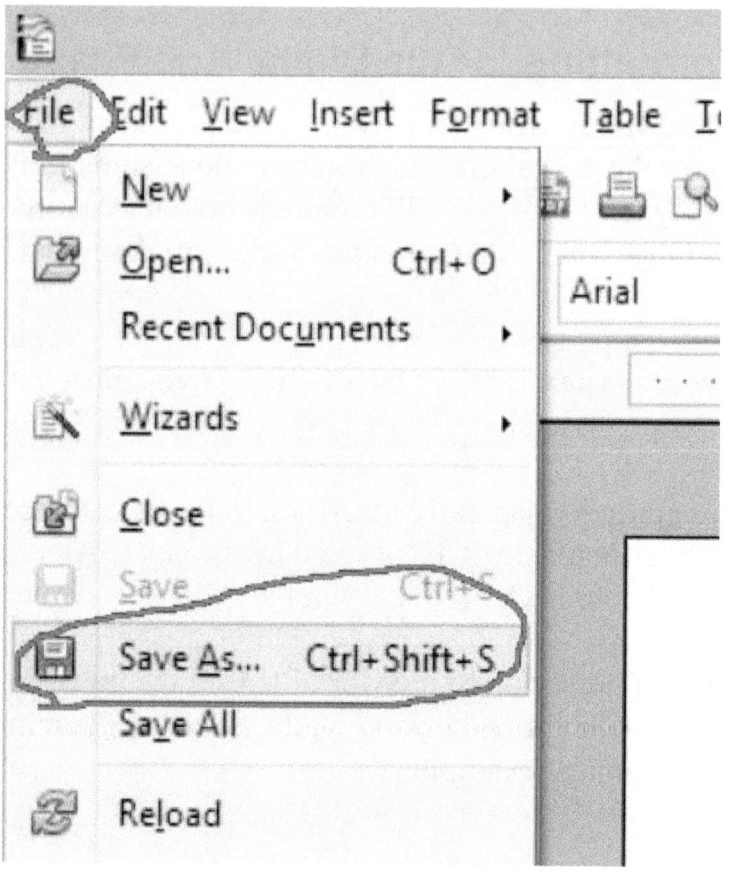

A new window will appear asking you where you would like to save your masterpiece. If you notice down towards the bottom of this window there are two drop down boxes. One is for the FILE NAME, the other says SAVE AS TYPE. Save it where you have been saving all of your work, click the SAVE AS TYPE drop down box and select HTML DOCUMENT (OPENOFFICE WRITER) (.HTML) (*.HTML). Then click the save button at the bottom. Use the handy image below for a guide.

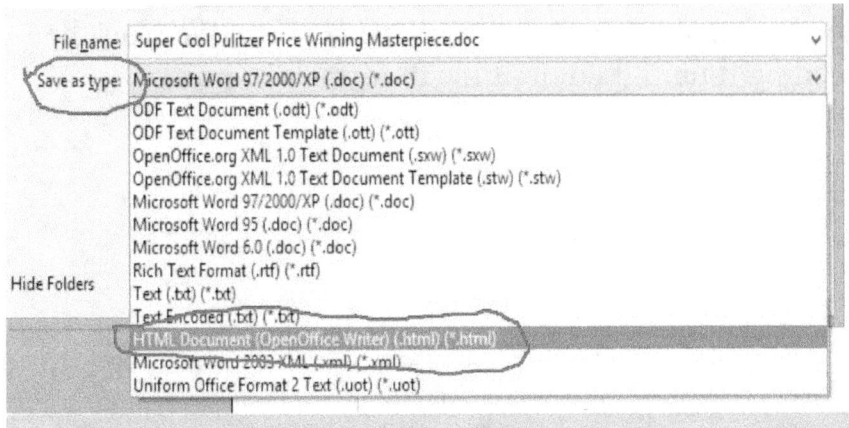

Open Office might prompt you with a warning box that look like the image below. Just click KEEP CURRENT FORMAT and move on.

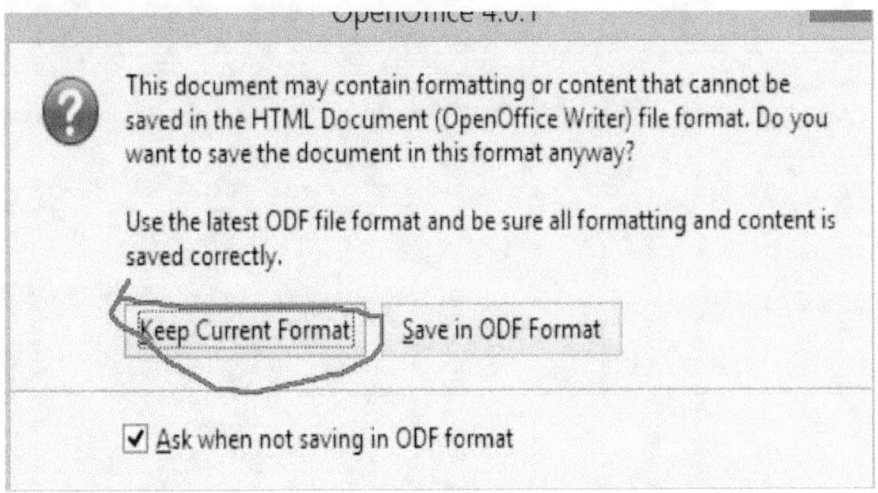

Congratulations! Your masterpiece has now been

magically transformed into a pretty handy HTML document. You can now close Open Office. We won't be needing it until it comes time to format for print.

Formatting With Calibre

All right it is time to learn something entirely new. There is a really good chance that you have never used this piece of software. If you have not downloaded and installed it yet, do it. You must have it if you want to achieve world domination and a perfectly formatted book suited for digital distribution. Here is the link again in case you missed it the first time.

http://calibre-ebook.com/

Find your copy of Calibre and open it. Ah! Look at all those shiny features. There are all kinds of buttons to push and settings to tweak. Are you ready? These are the final formatting steps. Here we go!

The first thing you want to do is locate the ADD BOOKS button in the upper left corner.

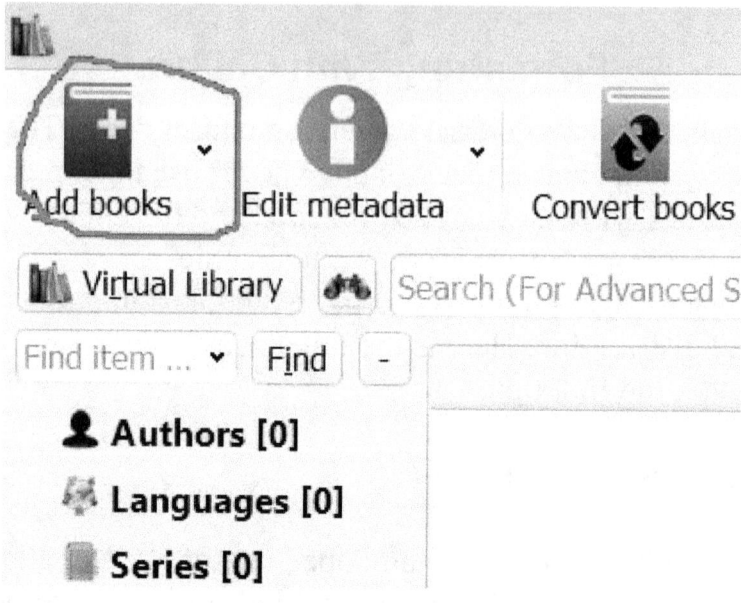

Go ahead and click it. A new window opens up prompting you for a file to add. Browse to the HTML version of your masterpiece and double click it. A new window should pop up telling you Calibre is adding your book. When it is done, your book should appear highlighted in the window below. Like this image.

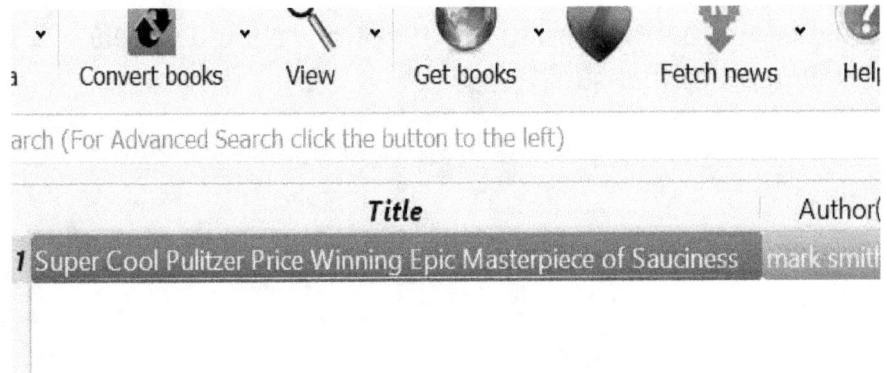

Let's put this little piece of software to work. If for any reason, your masterpiece is not highlighted. Click it once and it should be. If it still doesn't work. Open your computer, pour lighter fluid inside, strike a match and sacrifice it to the technology gods because something is seriously wrong with your machine.

Click the CONVERT BOOKS icon.

A new window with all kinds of options should appear. Look at all of that stuff!

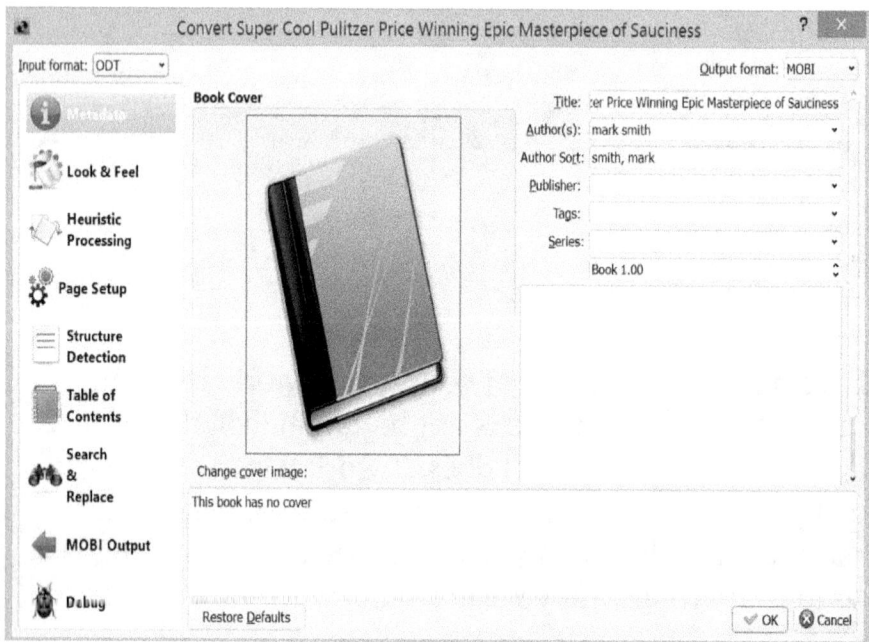

Don't let all those shiny buttons confuse you. We are only going to be using a few of them. The first and single most important lives in the upper right corner. It is labeled OUTPUT FORMAT. We need to change this so that it says EPUB.

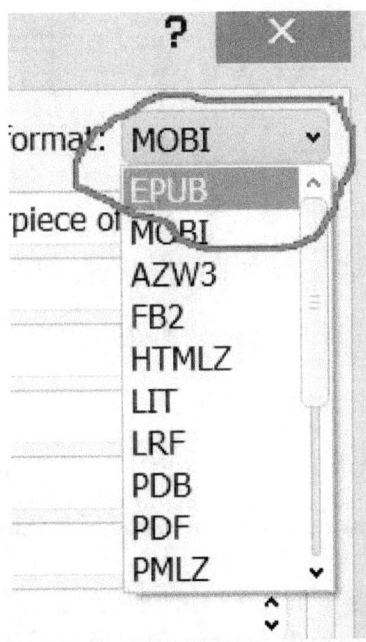

Once you have changed the format to EPUB, Look for the paint bucket on the left labeled: LOOK & FEEL. Go ahead and click it.

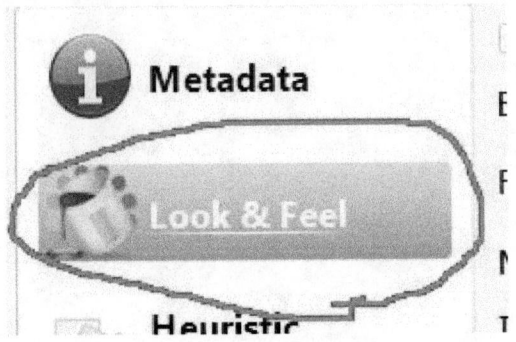

You should now be under the LOOK & FEEL options. There are only two things we are going to change here and one of them is a matter of personal preference. Tick the check box next to REMOVE SPACING BETWEEN PARAGRAPHS.

☐ Embed referenced fonts

☑ Remove spacing between paragraphs

☐ Insert blank line between paragraphs

Text justification:

☐ Smarten punctuation   ☐ Transliterate u

☐ UnSmarten punctuation   ☐ Keep ligatures

The next change is a personal preference. I don't like having every paragraph indented. I think it looks weird. If you don't mind, then skip this next piece. Here is how you remove the indent. Look for this.

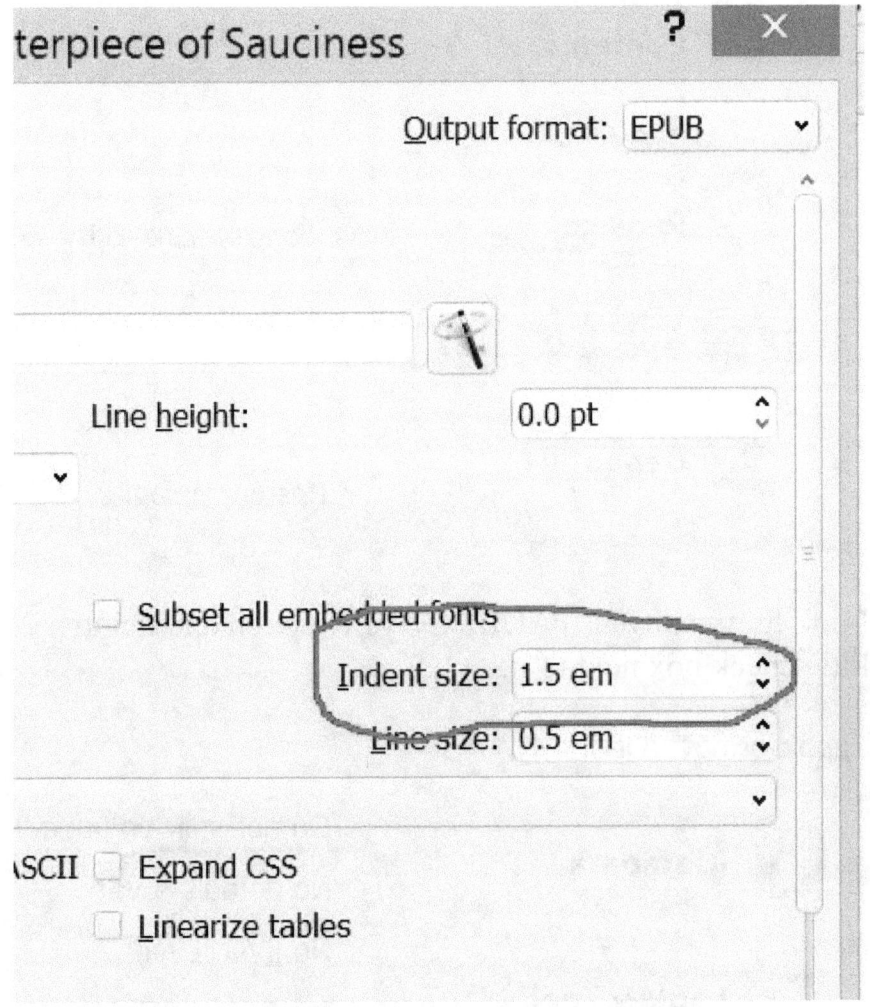

We want this INDENT SIZE to say 0.0 em. Change it and move on.

On the left menu look for EPUB OUTPUT and click it.

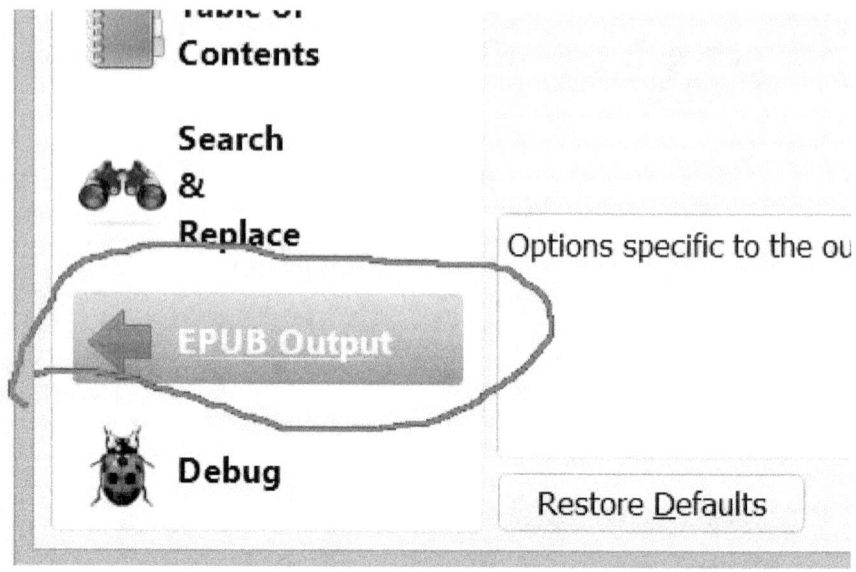

Look for the NO DEFAULT COVER option and tick the little check box next to it.

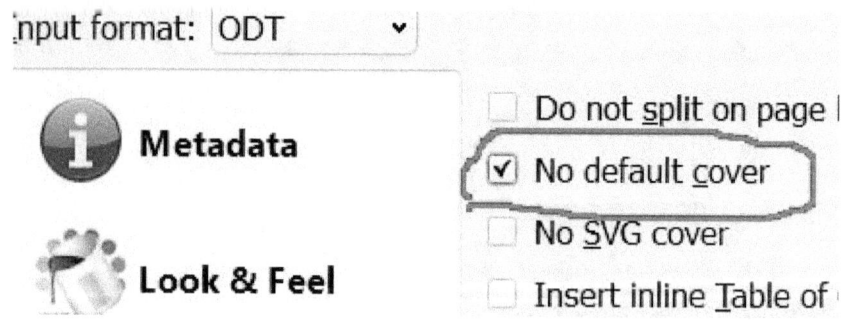

You are now ready to make Calibre go to work for you. Click the save button in the lower right corner. Calibre should now go to work converting your masterpiece. It may take a little while.

When the conversion process is done, your masterpiece should now be ready to upload to Amazon, but first you will have to find it. Calibre puts it in a special place. Look over to the right side underneath the big brown book. You are looking for an area that says: PATH CLICK TO OPEN. Here is an image for reference.

Click the words CLICK TO OPEN. This is the location of your newly transformed perfectly formatted masterpiece. Copy your masterpiece to the same location as the original ODT file you made in Open Office and remember where this is. You will need it when it comes time to upload to

Amazon.

That's it. You are all done. Your book is ready for the digital masses. All you need now is a great cover. The cover will make or break your book. Don't worry, I will show you how to get an awesome professional looking cover for just $5.00!

Getting A Professional Cover

One thing I have learned during my self publishing madness is this. A cover will sell a book on its own merit. The book could be complete and total garbage, but if the cover is perfection, then the book will sell faster than water in the desert. A bad cover has the exact opposite effect. A bad cover makes a book practically invisible.

You can choose to make your own cover. There is nothing wrong with this. You may even learn a thing or two. I know I did.

Designing a professional cover will require some really good software that can get quite expensive. When you are a success, you can dabble in cover design, but for now just pay someone to make you a great cover. You can get one created for a measly $5.00 at Fiverr.

Fiverr is a virtual marketplace where people offer you their services for a measly five dollars. At Fiverr the offering of services are labeled as a "gig." There are plenty of people who will be more than happy to create a cover that helps propel your book sales through the stratosphere.

Open up your favorite web browser and go to: http://www.fiverr.com.

Once you have arrived, do a quick search for the words

"book cover." You should get plenty of results. Go ahead and look through them. You should be able to see plenty of examples. Find one that suits your masterpiece and purchase the gig. Tell them you need the cover in a Kindle Ready format. Wait a few days, and your gig will be delivered. The cover for your masterpiece is ready and it only cost you $5.00! Rock on.

Here are the exact specifics as per Amazon regarding what will be needed from your cover. Hand this information over to whoever is creating the cover for your masterpiece.

"Kindle Direct Publishing accepts two types of files for cover images:

JPEG, or .jpeg
TIFF, or .tif(f)

KDP applies additional compression to images when displaying them on its website. For best results, please upload your images with minimal compression.

Dimensions

Requirements for the size of your cover art have an ideal height/width ratio of 1.6, this means:

• A minimum of 625 pixels on the shortest side and 1000 pixels on the longest side
• For best quality, your image would be 2820 pixels on the

shortest side and 4500 pixels on the longest side

Important: We cannot accept any image larger than 10,000 pixels on the longest side.

Color
Product images display on the Amazon website using RGB (red, green, blue) color mode. RGB is the color mode native to the web and many color screen displays, as these three colors displayed at varying levels of intensity create over 16 million colors.

Use color images whenever possible and relevant. The Kindle reading device has a black and white screen today but Kindle applications for other devices, such as iPhone or PC, take advantage of color fonts and images."

Kindle Direct Publishing

This is it. The moment you have been waiting for. It is time to SELF PUBLISH your very first book. If you don't already have a Kindle Direct Publishing account setup, now is the time to get one. Follow this link and get everything setup.

https://kdp.amazon.com/

If you already have an account with Amazon, then you can sign in using your existing account. Once you have your Kindle Direct Publishing account all setup and ready to go, click the little golden ADD NEW TITLE button. You will be magically transported to the Kindle Direct Publishing interface.

Amazon has extensive help throughout their dashboard. It would be pointless for me to repeat all of the information they have online explaining how to properly upload your book. However, I will give you some advice and highlight areas you should pay close attention to.

KDP Select

One of the first choices you need to make is whether or not to enroll your book in KDP Select. If you choose this option, you CAN'T sell a digital copy of your masterpiece anywhere else. Your masterpiece is exclusive to Amazon for the duration of this contract which is 90 days. Amazon does offer many benefits with this exclusivity and I have always chosen it at least for the first 90 days.

One of the benefits is the ability to give your book away for free for 5 days during the 90 day enrollment. This may sound like a stupid idea, but giving your book away for five days can help you get valuable reviews. It can also help your book climb all of the hot sales lists. There will be more eyes on your books. More eyes, means more sales. There is an entire marketing aspect to this that is beyond the scope of this book.

I am currently writing another epic masterpiece on how to successfully market your book. You can sign up to my mailing list to be the first to know about it. I also give free copies to those lucky enough to be on my mailing list. You can sign up here. It's free and I will only email you when I publish my new self publishing books.

http://eepurl.com/09Pq1

If after 90 days you no longer see any benefits of KDP

KDP Select

Select, then don't renew the contract.

There are other markets out there where you can sell digital copies of your masterpiece, but Amazon really does have the market cornered at the moment. I'm not saying your masterpiece won't sell in other locations. There is a really good chance it will, but Amazon should be your main focus for the moment.

Kindle Direct Publishing Description

The box labeled DESCRIPTION is very important. This is where you will be placing your insanely catchy synopsis.

If your cover looks good, this is usually the second place a reader will look. You already have the reader's attention so now you have to set the hook. Your synopsis has to be perfect. Most people tend to go overboard here, and there is nothing wrong with this. In fact, a longer synopsis filled with the right keywords can help your book be found, but and this is another big BUTT. (purposely misspelled that one) The first few lines of your synopsis have to be the most important.

Amazon does not display the entire synopsis to its readers. Why do you think this is? They have done extensive studies that have proven the first few sentences are the most important. In fact, Amazon makes you click a link labeled SHOW MORE to read the entire synopsis.

You may be thinking to yourself, that's no big deal. So you have to click a link to read the entire mouth watering, head spinning, super addictive synopsis. This is a HUGE deal. It takes a lot to get a person to click anything on the Internet and Amazon knows this. That is why they only display a small portion of the synopsis by default.

If you are lucky enough to entice a reader to click the

SHOW MORE link, then the reader has taken a liking to your synopsis. At this point, there is a really good chance they are going to make a purchase.

I am going to repeat myself and then show you a screen shot of the synopsis from one of my books. The first few lines are the **single most important** lines in the entire synopsis.

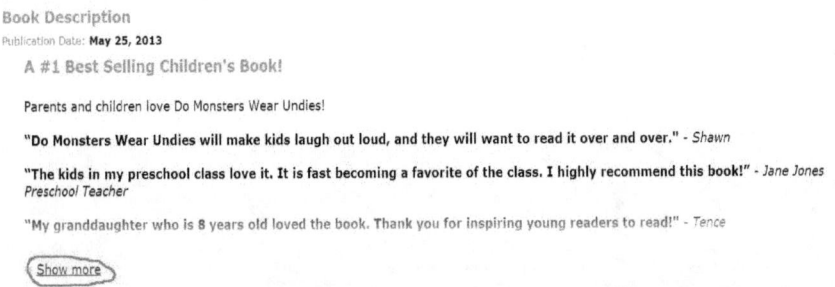

Notice the SHOW MORE link? All the somewhat boring stuff in the synopsis is hidden below that link. All the good stuff is right up front.
Now before you go create what you consider to be the best freaking synopsis in the world, you need to do a little bit of studying.

Head over to Amazon and locate a book that is similar to your masterpiece. Yeah I know, there is nothing that even comes close to what you have created, but there has got to be some more books that fall into the same genre. Look at the best selling books in these categories and study their synopsis. Don't copy them, but use them for inspiration.

If you know some HTML, you can use basic HTML code to make your synopsis look fancy like mine.

Kindle Direct Publishing Categories

You only get to choose two categories for your masterpiece and you had better choose them wisely. One of the most common problems people face in this situation is this. The categories in the Kindle Direct Publishing dashboard DO NOT mirror the categories on Amazon.com. In most cases, they are completely different. Do you think this will cause confusion? You bet it will, but don't panic; at least not yet.

Browse through all the categories. There is a really good chance that you will find two that fit your masterpiece like a glove. Awesome, choose them and wait for the royalties to come rolling in.

If for some reason you are having a difficult time locating the perfect categories, there is an option for you. It can be a little tricky, but the results are always outstanding. I have learned you always need to work a little to get to the good things in life. Its just the way things work. Here is what you need to do.

Click on the categories and scroll all the way down to the bottom. You are looking for the NON-CLASSIFIABLE category. Click the box next to NON-CLASSIFIABLE and click save. Check out the picture below.

Kindle Direct Publishing Categories

You fool! You have fallen for my trap. Now your book will never sell a single copy. This has been my master plan all along and you fell for it. HA HA HA!

Enough of the evil persona dude. Having your book reside in this category can actually be beneficial. Here's why.

It may be easier to locate a book that is similar to yours on Amazon and take note of the category. You may have never done this before. Here's what you need to do. Follow this link. It is a link to one of my best selling children's books. If you have kids, you may want to buy this book for them. I have been told it is pretty entertaining!

http://www.amazon.com/Do-Monsters-Wear-Undies-Childrens-ebook/dp/B00D0S8NOY/

Scroll down towards the bottom of the page and look for this.

Product Details

File Size: 2442 KB

Print Length: 41 pages

Simultaneous Device Usage: Unlimited

Sold by: Amazon Digital Services, Inc.

Language: English

ASIN: B00D0S8NOY

Text-to-Speech: Enabled ☑

X-Ray: Not Enabled ☑

Lending: Enabled

Amazon Best Sellers Rank: #18,135 Paid in Kindle Store (See Top 100 Paid in Kindle Store)
  #4 in Kindle Store > Kindle eBooks > Children's eBooks > Humor > **Jokes & Riddles**
  #9 in Books > Children's Books > Humor > **Jokes & Riddles**
  #39 in Kindle Store > Kindle eBooks > Children's eBooks > Literature & Fiction > **Beginner Readers**

See the part in the big red circle? Those are the categories. Only pay attention to the ones that start with KINDLE STORE. The other is for the paperback version.

Now you need to find a book that is similar to your masterpiece and locate its categories. If the book is not selling well, Amazon will not display any categories.

Once you find a book that is similar to yours and it is selling well, copy the exact category structure. In my example there would be these two.

Kindle Store > Kindle eBooks > Children's eBooks >
Humor > Jokes & Riddles
Kindle Store > Kindle eBooks > Children's eBooks >
Literature & Fiction > Beginner Readers

Now you need to inform the great people who work at
Kindle Direct Publishing these are the two categories
where you would like to see your masterpiece reside. This
is yet another easy process. Here is what you need to do.

Log into your Amazon Kindle Direct publishing account.
Once you have signed into your account, follow this link:

**https://kdp.amazon.com/help?
topicId=A200PDGPEIQX41**

From here scroll down and look for the golden CONTACT
US button on the left.

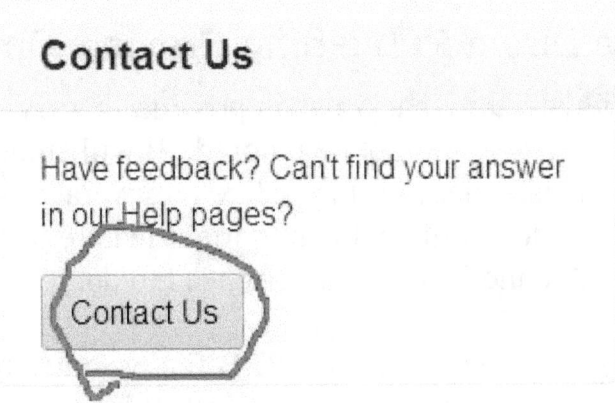

You will now be presented with an option to contact the team at Kindle Direct Publishing and tell them about your categories dilemma. They will want to know the exact category path you would like your masterpiece to be in. I already told you to copy these.

Write your note to the team, answer any questions that may already be in the contact box and tell them you want your book to be in the categories you have selected. If you did everything correctly, then you should get an email back from them within 48 hours telling you everything is ready to go.

Kindle Direct Publishing Preview Options

The preview feature that Amazon provides is very powerful and it should not be ignored. It will emulate what your masterpiece will look like on several devices. A lot of people don't utilize this important feature. I highly recommend it and here's what you need to do.

The first step is to upload the EPUB file we made using Open Office and Calibre. Amazon calls this your book content file. When you upload your book, Amazon converts it to the Kindle ready format. This is a MOBI file. Once the online conversion is complete, you get the option to preview your masterpiece on a multitude of devices. Here is what you need to look for.

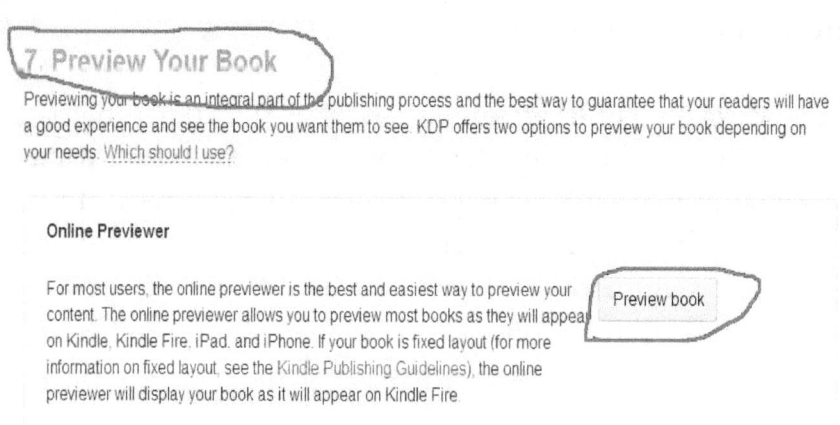

7. Preview Your Book

Previewing your book is an integral part of the publishing process and the best way to guarantee that your readers will have a good experience and see the book you want them to see. KDP offers two options to preview your book depending on your needs. Which should I use?

Online Previewer

For most users, the online previewer is the best and easiest way to preview your content. The online previewer allows you to preview most books as they will appear on Kindle, Kindle Fire, iPad, and iPhone. If your book is fixed layout (for more information on fixed layout, see the Kindle Publishing Guidelines), the online previewer will display your book as it will appear on Kindle Fire.

Preview book

Click the PREVIEW BOOK button and be magically transferred to Amazon's online book emulation. There is a menu system that appears on top of the emulation section of the site. There is one portion of the menu that is the most important. It is labeled: DEVICE. This is where you can choose to emulate what your masterpiece will look like.

Click it and experiment with all of the different devices available.

Kindle Direct Publishing Pricing

Pricing your masterpiece for the Kindle is not very straight forward. If your masterpiece is enrolled in KDP Select, readers have the ability to borrow your book. You get paid for these borrows. At the time of this writing, borrows averaged around $2.00 a piece.

Amazon recently announced a new subscription service that costs readers $9.99 per month. Readers who subscribe to this service can download and read as many books as their hungry little brains can consume. The books must be enrolled in KDP Select. Authors get paid for this service when a reader downloads their book and reads it past 10%. The amount of the payment has yet to be determined. It works on averages and a sliding scale.

You will also get paid when someone purchases your masterpiece. The total amount of money that hits your bank account will vary on a few things.

The sales price of your masterpiece determines the overall percentage you net. If your masterpiece is $2.99 or more, you will earn a 70% royalty minus the delivery fee. When you set the price for your masterpiece, Amazon will show you an estimated delivery fee.

If you price your book below the $2.99 pricing point, your royalty drops to 35%. It may seem like a no brainer to shoot for the higher royalty payment, but with the 35% royalty payout, Amazon does not charge a delivery fee. If your masterpiece is image heavy, you may actually make more profit going for the lower royalty.

Do the math to determine which payment structure will bring you the most profit and world domination will soon be yours!

That is all there is to it. If you did everything correctly, you should now be in self publishing limbo while Amazon reviews your masterpiece. As long as your masterpiece isn't some content that you copied from another source, it should be ready for the masses in as little as 12 hours!

Congratulations. Go out and smoke a cigar, drink some champagne, wine, beer or do whatever it is you do to celebrate. You are now a self published author, but now it is time to take that same masterpiece and put it in paperback format.

Are you ready for the challenge? Do you want to make more book sales? Then you need to make sure your book is available in paperback format too!

Formatting For Print

Having your book available in print is never a bad idea. You already spent countless hours slaving over your masterpiece. You might as well squeeze that lemon until it is dry, right? I am not implying your masterpiece is a lemon. It could be an orange, a lime or a strawberry. The point I am trying to make is this. REPURPOSE YOUR CONTENT and prosper. You decided to try your hand at self publishing so that you could achieve freedom and world domination right? Well this is one very powerful step towards getting there.

Formatting for print is like stepping into a brave new world. We are going to be covering all types of things you may have never heard of, but if you made it through the Kindle formatting section, then this should be as simple as drinking a glass of milk. Unless of course you are lactose intolerant. If you are lactose intolerant then this will be as simple as pie. Unless you are diabetic. OK FORGET IT! It will be easy. Get the coffee brewing and get ready to launch your writing career to a new level.

Createspace

Createspace is a print on demand company owned by Amazon. It is here where we will be moving your masterpiece to the paperback world, and we will be using Open Office to format the interior to perfection. You will even be able to use your original ODT file that you used for digital distribution. We will need to make some serious changes to it for print though.

Open your favorite web browser and head over to: www.createspace.com

Sign up and create a new account there. Take care of all the formalities to ensure your hard earned royalties end up in your bank account. Once you are done with that, it is time to get your masterpiece ready for print. Look for the big blue button in your createspace dashboard labeled ADD NEW TITLE, and click it. It looks like this.

Add New Title

A new window should appear asking you for the name of your project, and what type of product you would like to create. Ewww! Look at all those choices.

Createspace

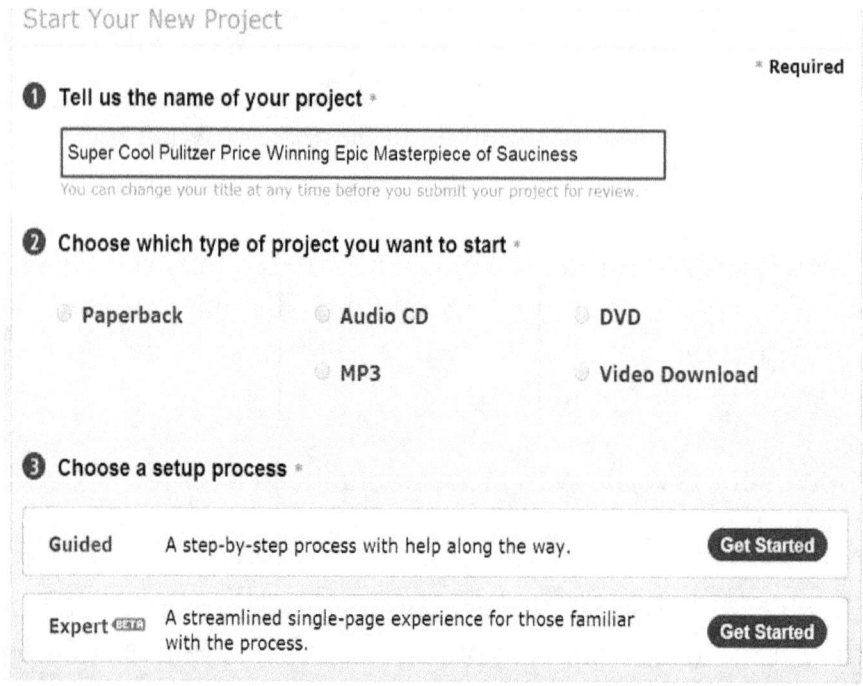

I bet you didn't know you could make a paperback, an audio CD, an MP3 file, a DVD or a Video Download. Just think of the endless possibilities here.

For now, choose paperback and then pay close attention to the two GET STARTED options. Which one do you think you should pick? Guided or Expert? Let's go with guided for the first few times.

As soon as you click GET STARTED, things are going to get somewhat familiar. Look at that. They want to know the title of your masterpiece, the author name and everything else you already had to fill out when you uploaded your masterpiece for digital distribution through the Kindle. Only three fields are required. They are: TITLE, PRIMARY AUTHOR and LANGUAGE.

If you look over to the left, you will be able to see your overall progress indicator like the image below.

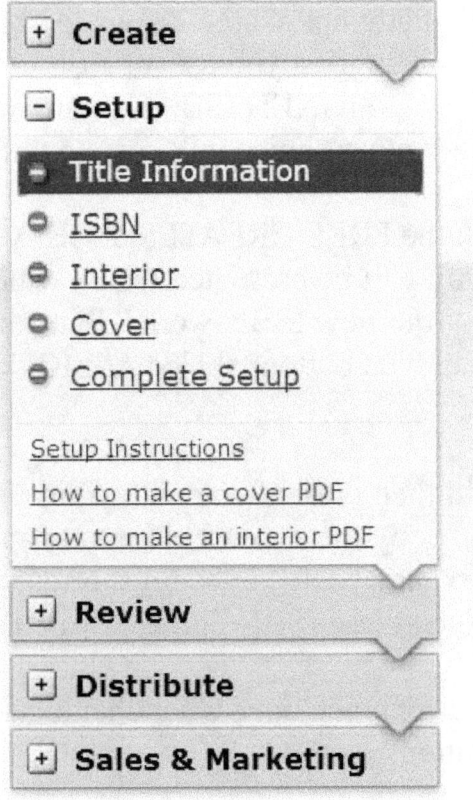

Fill out all of the title information and click the big blue SAVE & CONTINUE button. Notice the progress on the left has now changed. The Title information should now have a green check mark next to it.

You are now on the ISBN page. This part will require some decisions from you. You have four choices, and Createspace does a good job of detailing the differences in all four choices.

If this is your first attempt at creating a paperback masterpiece, then I suggest you use a FREE CREATESPACE-ASSIGNED ISBN. We are doing things cheap here. Every other choice will cost you money.

When you click the FREE CREATESPACE-ASSIGNED ISBN option, you will be presented with a window explaining how your new ISBN works. Read all of it and then click the big blue button labeled ASSIGN FREE ISBN.

Createspace will then present you with your brand new ISBN numbers. Copy these down either on paper or using those handy copy and paste keyboard shortcuts I taught you. You will need these ISBN numbers when we work on the interior.
You only have one choice now. Click that big blue CONTINUE button.

Now for the fun part. We get to make some really serious choices. Createspace does an excellent job here of informing you about all of these choices. Createspace wants your book to be successful. They get paid when your book sells.

Unless your book is an image heavy children's book that requires full color printing, go with all the default settings Createspace gives you on this page. You can't click save yet because you don't have a print ready interior PDF file. Can you guess what we need to do next?

Creating A Print Ready PDF File

Now for the fun part. You are going to magically transform your original masterpiece that you formatted for digital distribution. The first step is simple. We are going to be using the SAVE AS feature of Open Office This will allow you to save a new copy of your masterpiece without messing up the original. Pretty smart huh? Here is how you do it.

Click FILE → SAVE AS. You will be prompted with a new SAVE AS dialog box. Make sure you save your file in the same location as your old one, but you must give it a different name.

I like to prefix my file names with the words FOR-PRINT. This makes it easier to locate and determine which file is which. So name your new file something like FOR-PRINT-epic-masterpiece.odt and click the save button. We now have a new copy of your masterpiece that we can tweak and change for print.

Now it is time to make some serious changes to the formatting of your masterpiece. Keep in mind the following settings will only work if you have chosen the default book size of 6x9 that Createspace suggested for you.

Click FORMAT and then click PAGE.

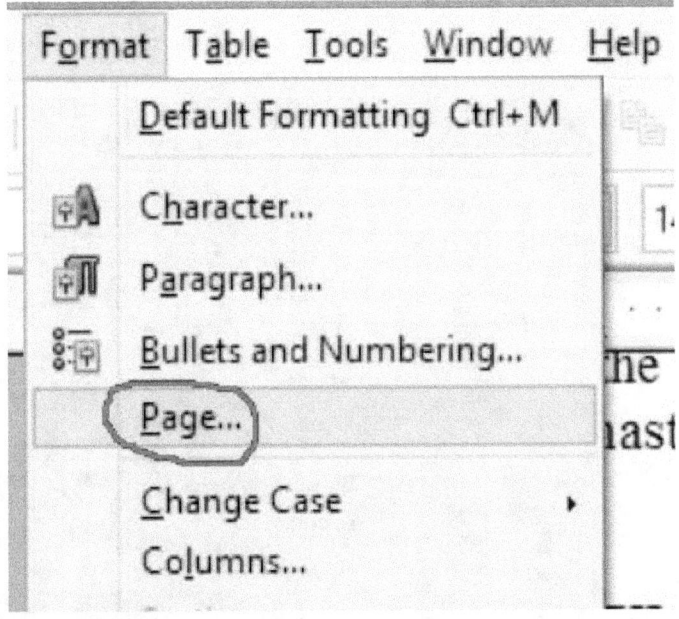

The page formatting window should magically appear. This part is crucial! One wrong setting and your entire masterpiece will be destroyed. Not really, but it will look really messed up.

If you chose the default text file for Open Office like I suggested in the very beginning, your setting should look exactly like this.

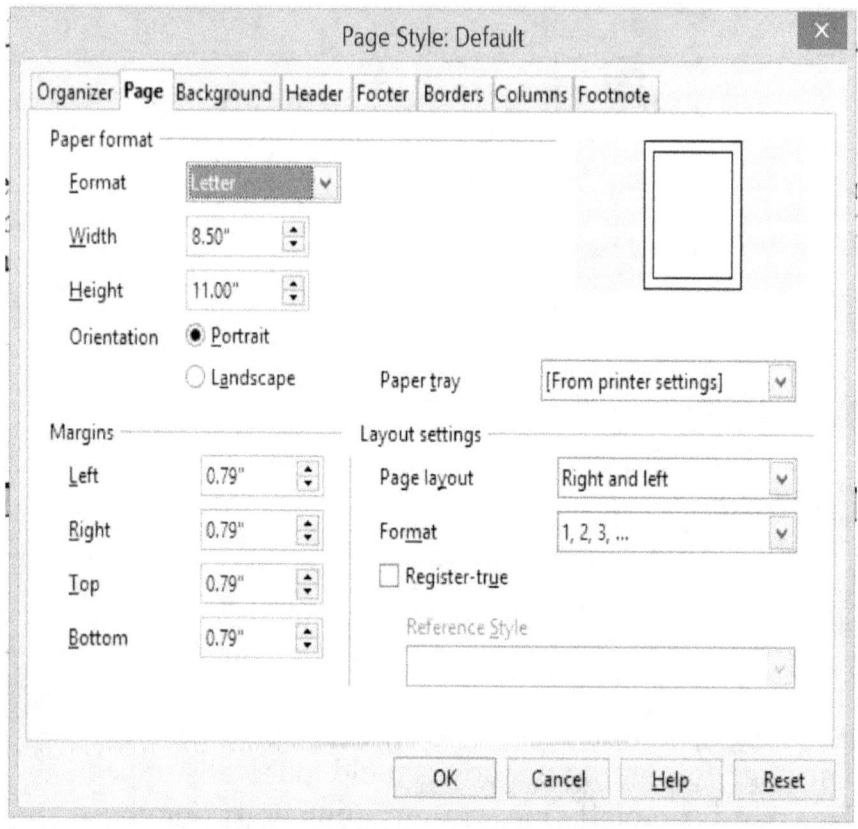

The first thing that needs to be changed is the format. Change it to user like the image below.

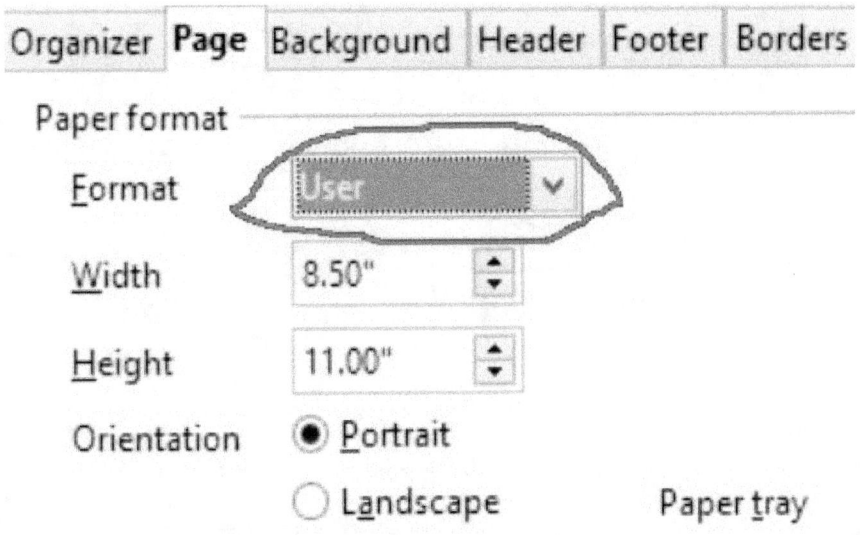

Now we need to change the width to 6.00" and the height the 9.00" like the image below.

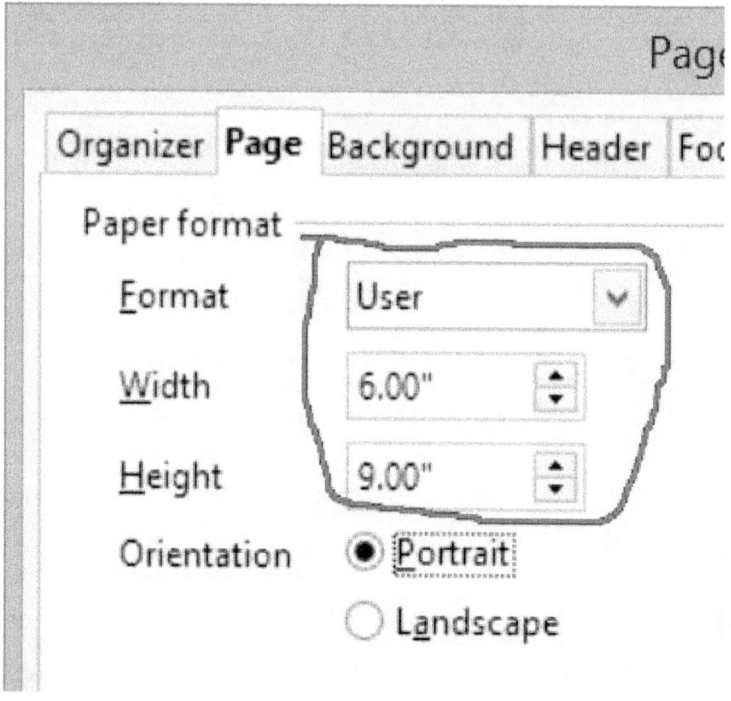

Next you need to change the PAGE LAYOUT option from RIGHT AND LEFT to MIRRORED like the image below.

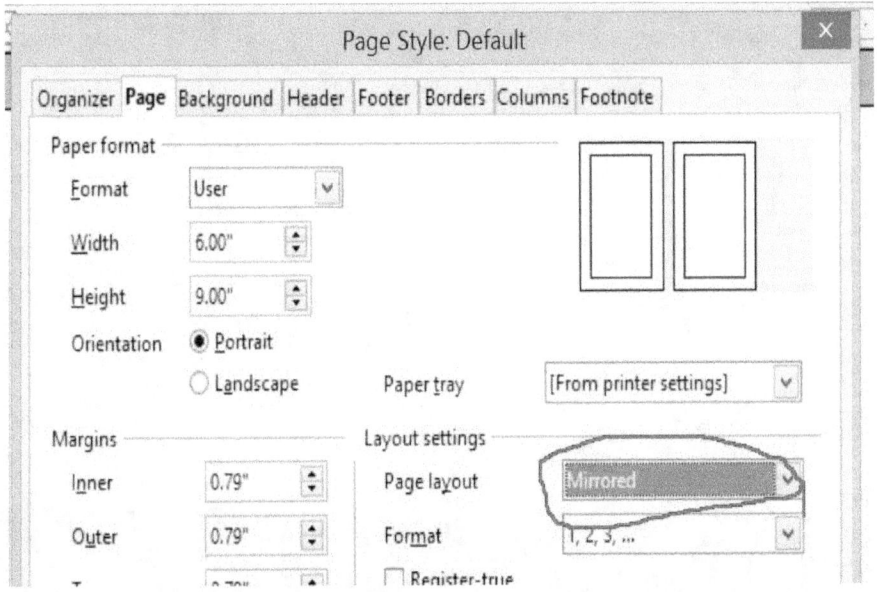

Changing the PAGE LAYOUT to MIRRORED will automatically change some of the options under MARGINS. It doesn't change the measurements under MARGINS. It changes the actual areas where you can make adjustments which is very important. Now we need to change the margins to say the following.

Inner: 0.88"
Outer: 0.50"
Top: 0.75"
Bottom: 0.75"

Use the image below for reference.

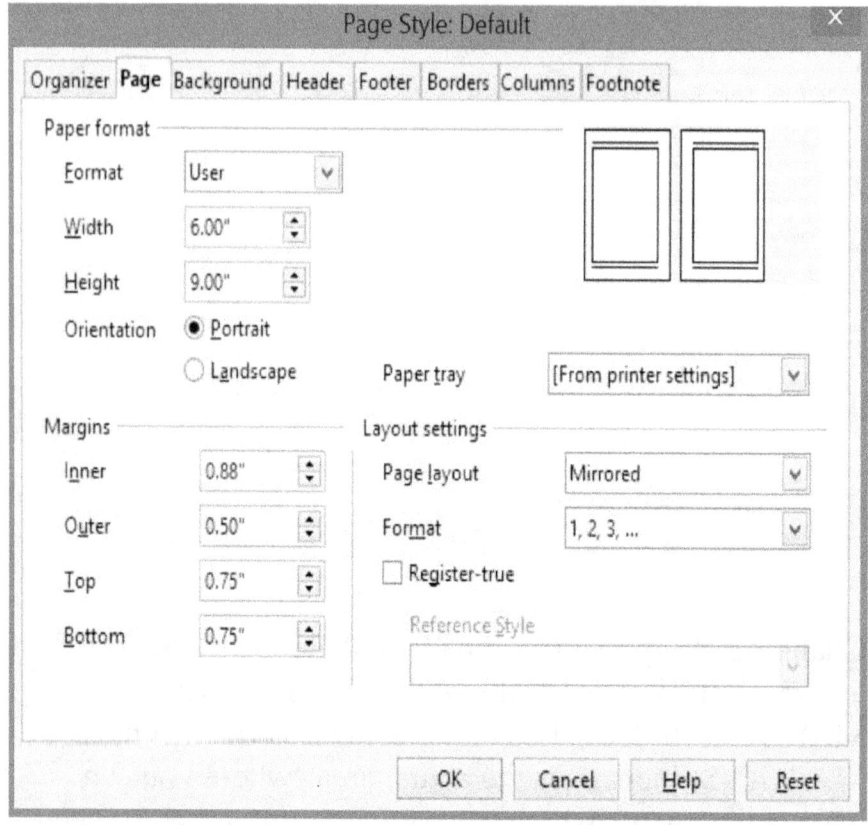

Don't click OK just yet. We have one more setting to make. Click the HEADER tab in the PAGE FORMATTING window like the image below.

Creating A Print Ready PDF File

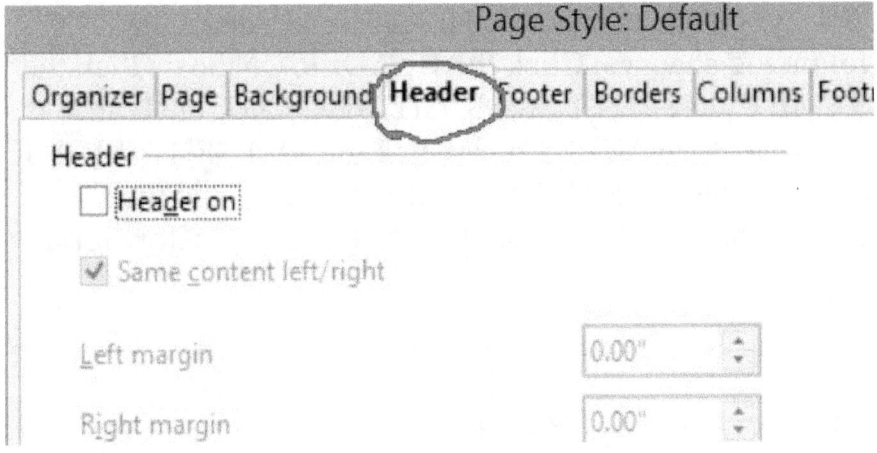

Once you have clicked the HEADER tab, make the following changes. Click the HEADER ON box. Click the SAME CONTENT LEFT/RIGHT box. Click the USE DYNAMIC SPACING box. Click the AUTOFIT HEIGHT box. Change the SPACING option to 0.35", and then change the HEIGHT to 0.04". Use the image below for a reference.

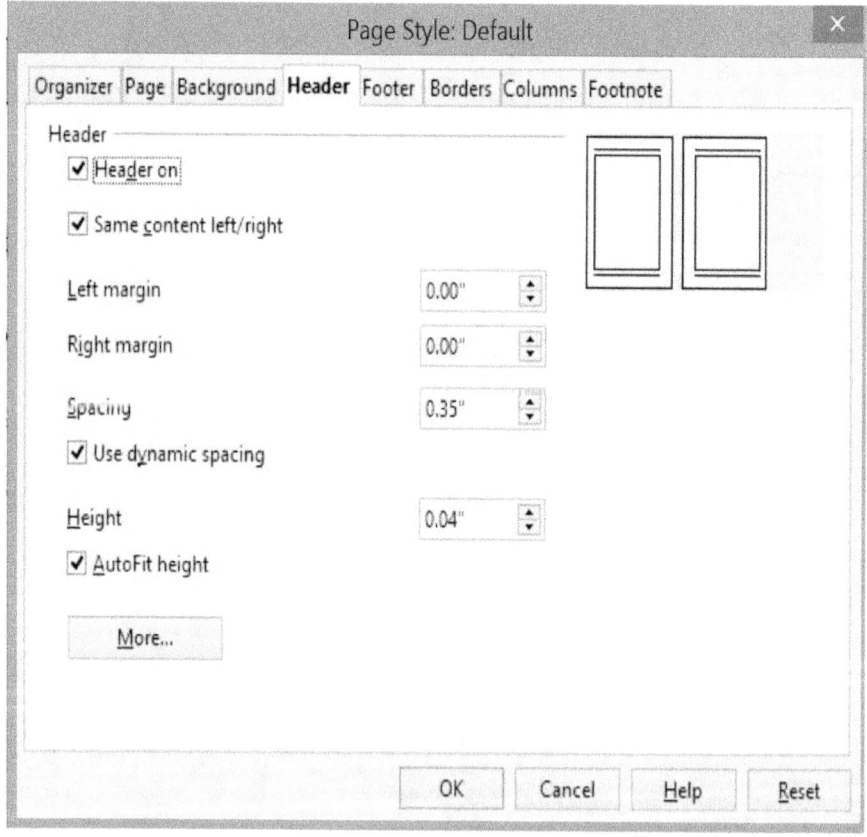

Now we need to add a footer to your masterpiece. Click the FOOTER tab. It is located right next to the HEADER tab. Click the FOOTER ON box. Click the SAME CONTENT LEFT/RIGHT box. Click the USE DYNAMIC SPACING box. Click the AUTOFIT HEIGHT box. Change the SPACING option to 0.35", and then change the HEIGHT to 0.04". These are the same settings we used for the header setup. Use the image below for a reference.

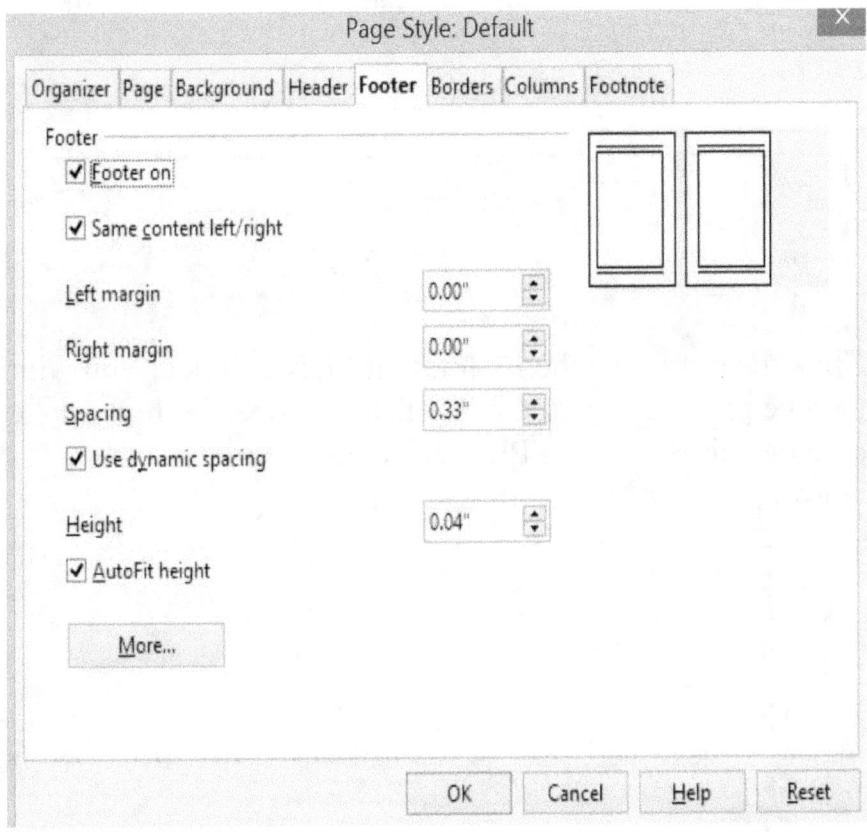

Now you are ready to click the OK button and watch your

masterpiece magically transform right before your eyes. Hopefully nothing weird happened. If your masterpiece uses images, they will need to be re-sized because they are now beyond the borders we just set. Unfortunately you will need to do this manually, but it is fairly easy. Here's how it is done.

Click an image in your masterpiece. The IMAGE PROPERTIES box should magically appear. It looks like this:

Click the button on the far left that I have circled. You will then be presented with the PICTURE properties box. Make sure the tab labeled TYPE is selected like in the image below.

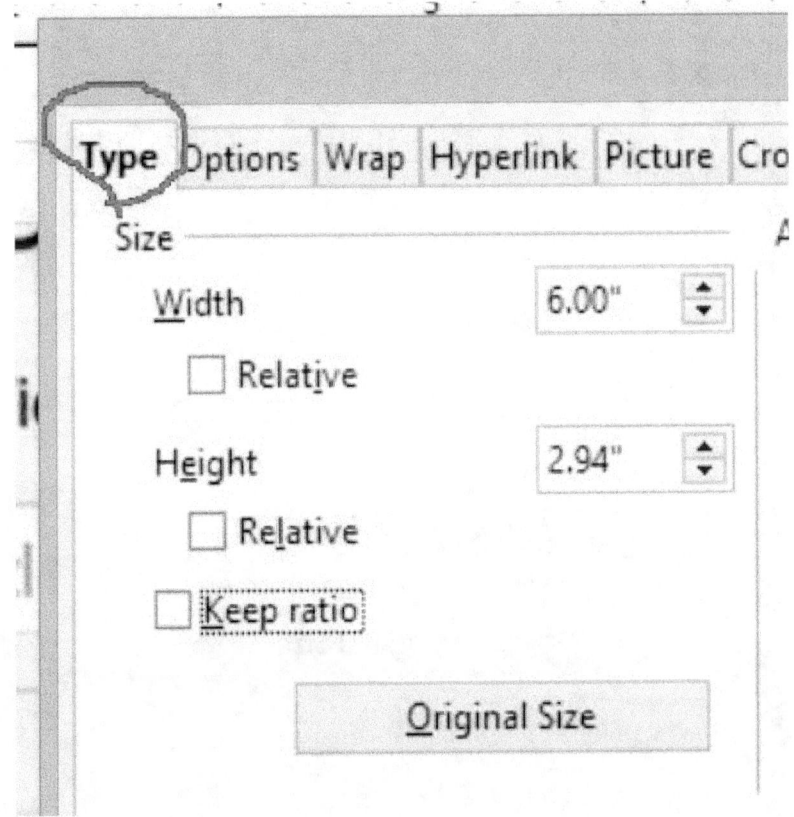

Now you need to click the RELATIVE box under width, the RELATIVE box under height and the KEEP RATIO box. It should look like this.

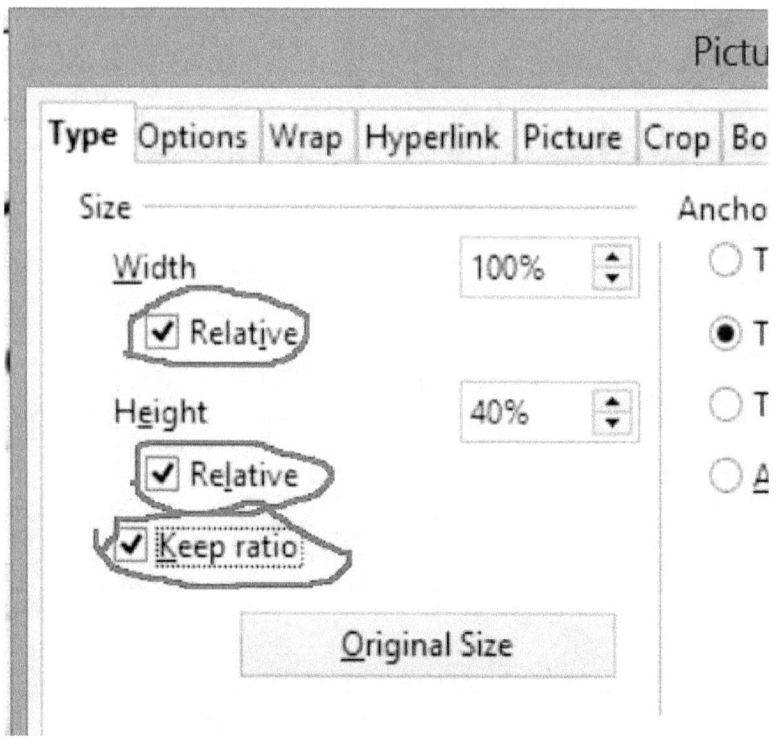

With everything checked off, click the OK button and your image should now fit within the borders of the page. You will need to do this to every image in your masterpiece.

Title and Legal Page for Print

Now let's move back to the title page because we need to make some changes here. We are going to move all of the legal information to its own page. The title page for your print masterpiece should only show the Title and the author. We also need to add our ISBN numbers to the new legal page.

Delete everything on the title page but the title and the author byline. Click underneath the author name. Your cursor should be blinking under the author name. Now it is time to insert a new blank page for the legal info. Do you remember how to do that? Hold down the "ctrl" key, while you are holding the "ctrl" key down press the "enter" key. You should now have a new blank page for your legal info.

Use a size 10 font and arrange all the information on your legal page to look like the image below. Replace all my information with yours. This gives your book that extra professional look to it.

ISBN-13: 978-1500783686
ISBN-10: 1500783684
Super Cool Pulitzer Price Winning Epic Masterpiece of Sauciness

Copyright 2014 and Beyond All Rights Reserved
Mark Smith

No part of this book may be reproduced, copied, or transmitted in any form without the written consent of the author.

Table of Contents for Print

We are almost done. Now we need to rebuild the table of contents. We need to remove the hyperlinks we added for the digital version and then we need to add the page numbers. Find your current table of contents and RIGHT CLICK anywhere inside it. You should see a window like this. Click EDIT INDEX/TABLE.

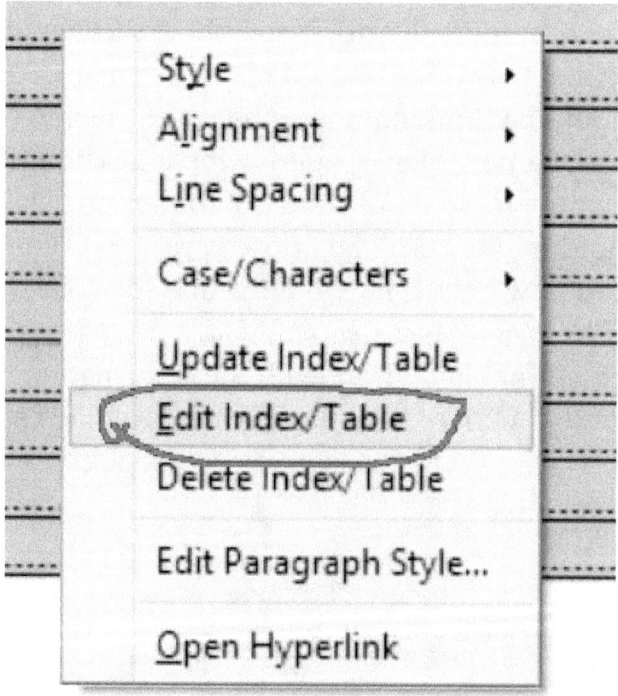

For the first step, let's remove those hyperlinks we added. This is really simple. Click the LS button in the table of contents window and then press the DELETE key on your keyboard. Use the image below for reference.

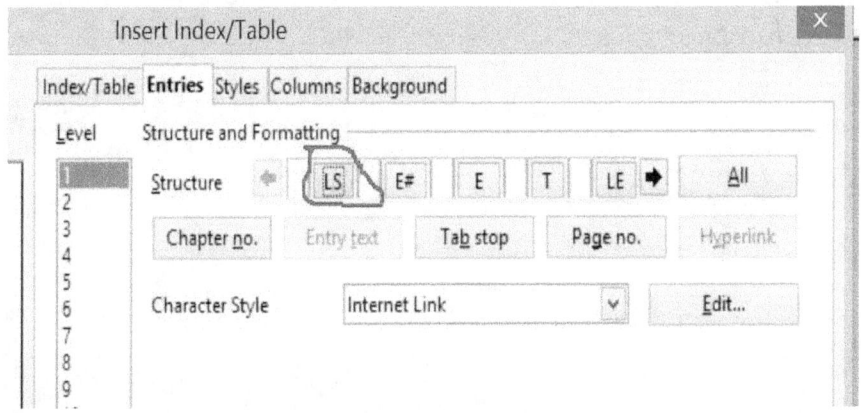

Once it is gone, do the same exact thing to the LE button. Click it and then press DELETE on your keyboard. You should now see this.

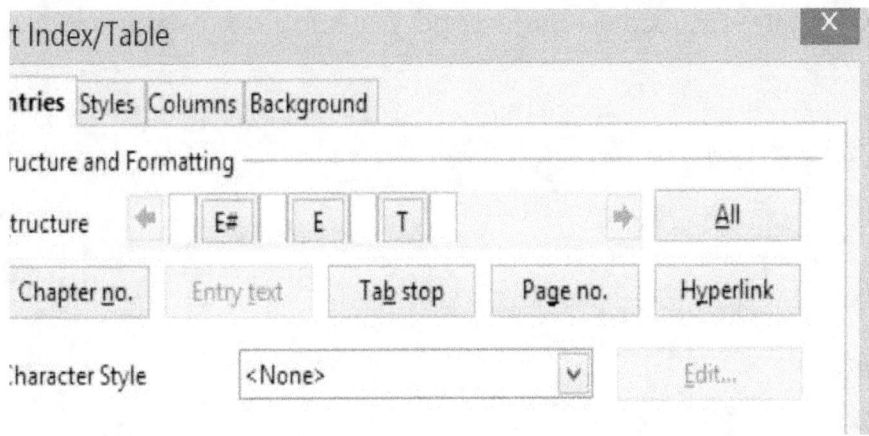

Your cursor should now be blinking right behind the T

button. It is taunting you. It wants you to do something. If your cursor is not blinking right next to the T button. Click that tiny space right next to the T button. Here is an image for reference.

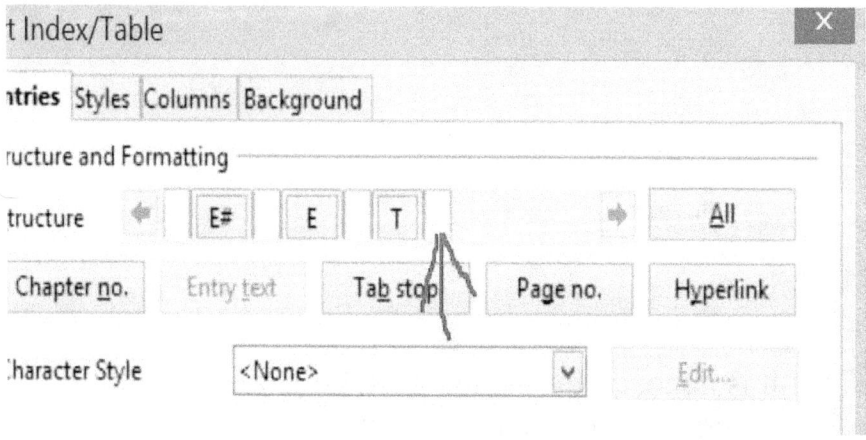

Now your cursor should be flashing next to the T button. Click the PAGE NO button and you should now see this.

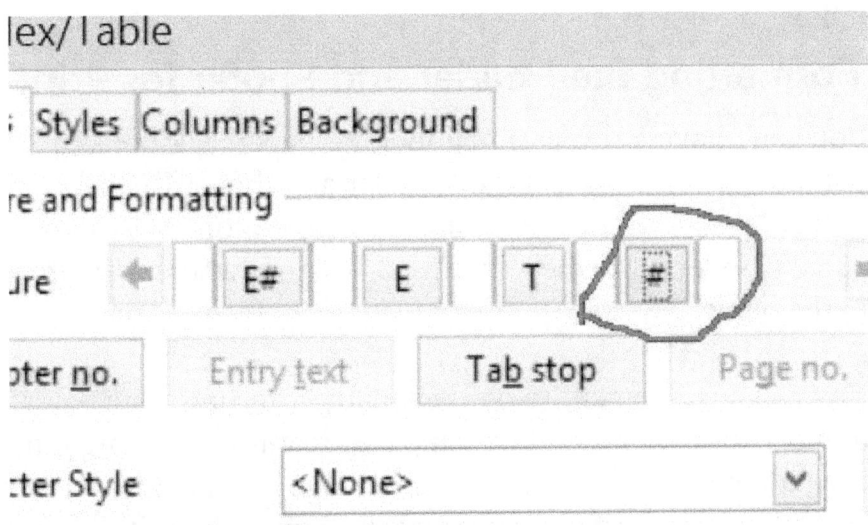

Now all you need to do is click that magic OK button and your table of contents should be rebuilt complete with page numbers.

If you need to make any updates or changes to your table of contents, RIGHT CLICK anywhere in the table of contents and click EDIT INDEX/TABLE.

If you make any changes to your masterpiece that might reflect inaccuracies in your table of contents, RIGHT CLICK anywhere in your table of contents and click UPDATE INDEX/TABLE. Now one final step and your masterpiece will be ready for print.

Formatting the Header and Footer for Print

You can't have a professional looking paperback book without a properly formatted header and footer. Readers will at least expect page numbers at the bottom of every page. How else are they supposed to know where they are in the book?

You can spend an entire day manually inserting page numbers at the bottom of each page. Just imagine how fun it would be to make changes to the page numbers if something should fall out of whack. Forget about it. Open Office provides a handy automated page inserting process. Here is what you need to do.

You should see a small rectangle at the bottom of every page. When we setup the footer, this magically appeared. It should look like this.

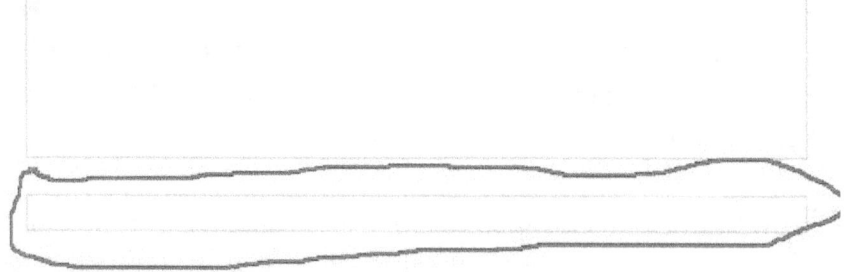

Click in this rectangle and you should once again see that flashing taunting cursor. By default the cursor on my masterpiece appears left justified. I don't like this. Page numbers should be in the center. This means we need to click the CENTER justify button in the formatting toolbar up top. It looks like this.

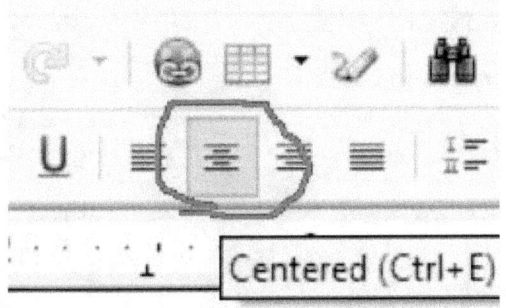

Now the annoying blinking cursor should be centered. Click INSERT->FEILDS->PAGE NUMBER. Here is an image for reference.

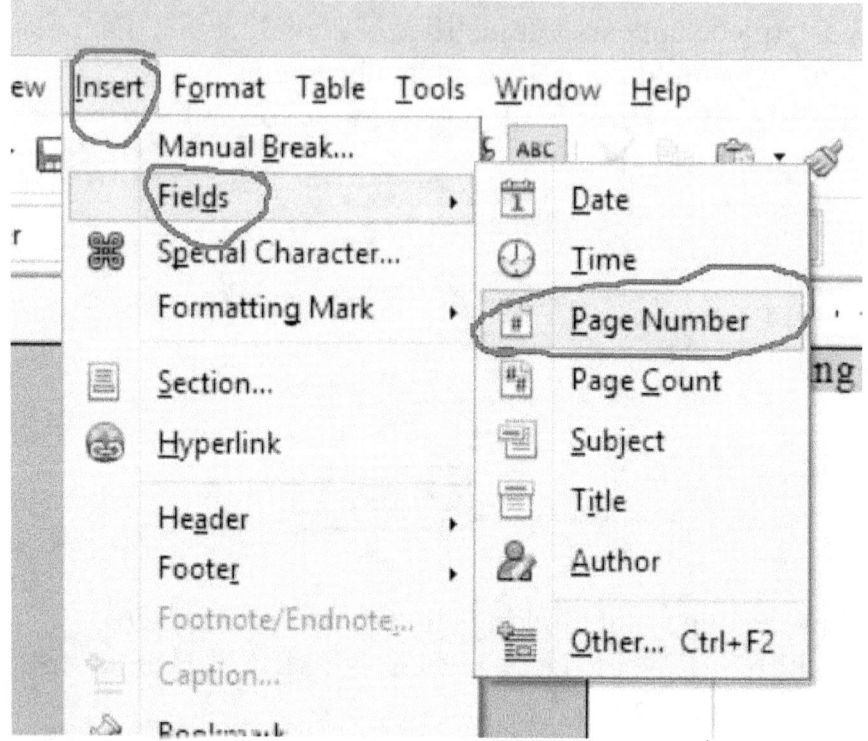

Page numbers should now magically appear at the bottom of every page! Now let's add the chapter name to the header of every page. Once again Open Office has a wonderful option that automates the entire process.

Adding chapter titles in the header works very similar to adding page numbers in the footer, but we have to dig a little deeper to get the chapter titles option.

Navigate to the first page of your masterpiece, not the title page and not the table of contents. Once you have found the first page click in the little header box that appears at the top of each page. Here is an image example.

Introduction

There is something really incredible about pouring your heart and soul into your first masterpiece and seeing it

Make sure your little blinking cursor is center justified. We already went over doing this twice. You should know how to do this by now. Wink Wink.

Once your blinking cursor is properly centered, click INSERT->FEILDS->OTHER. Use the image below for reference.

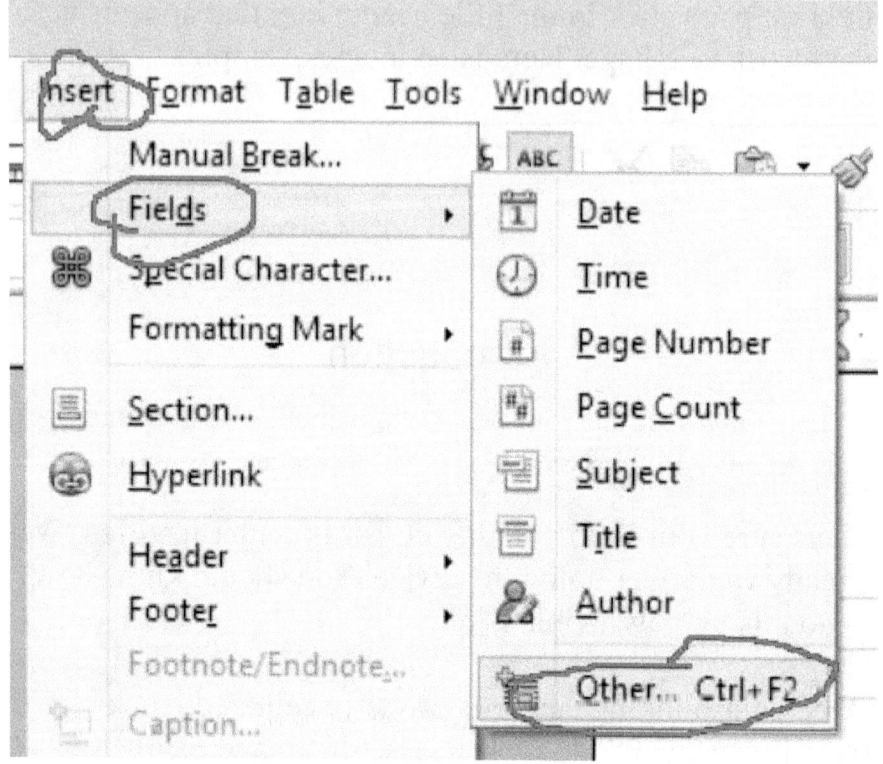

You will now see this handy dandy window.

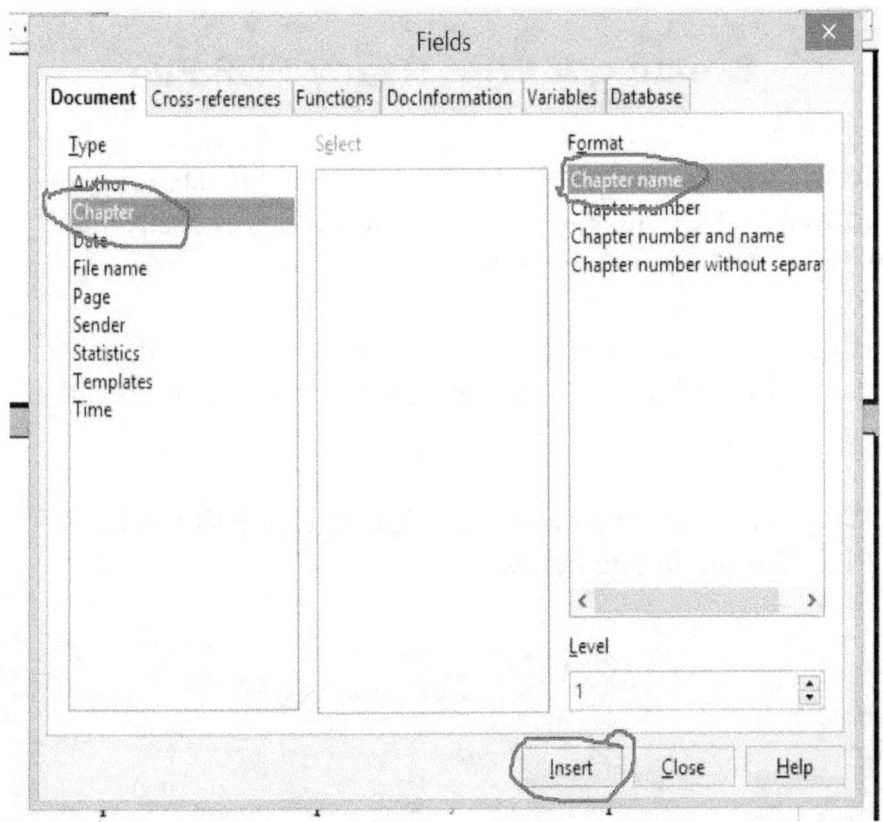

Click the word CHAPTER, then click CHAPTER NAME, then click INSERT, then click CLOSE.

You should now have the chapter name listed in the header of every single page. Congratulations your masterpiece is now formatted for print. Click FILE->SAVE.

Creating A Print Ready PDF File

What a minute? I thought you said my masterpiece was formatted for print? It is, but now we need to save it in a format that Createspace wants. Don't worry it is short and simple, but it has to be done.

If you still have your masterpiece open in Open Office, then let's get busy. If you don't have it open, then open that sucka.

With your masterpiece open, Click FILE->EXPORT AS PDF like the image below.

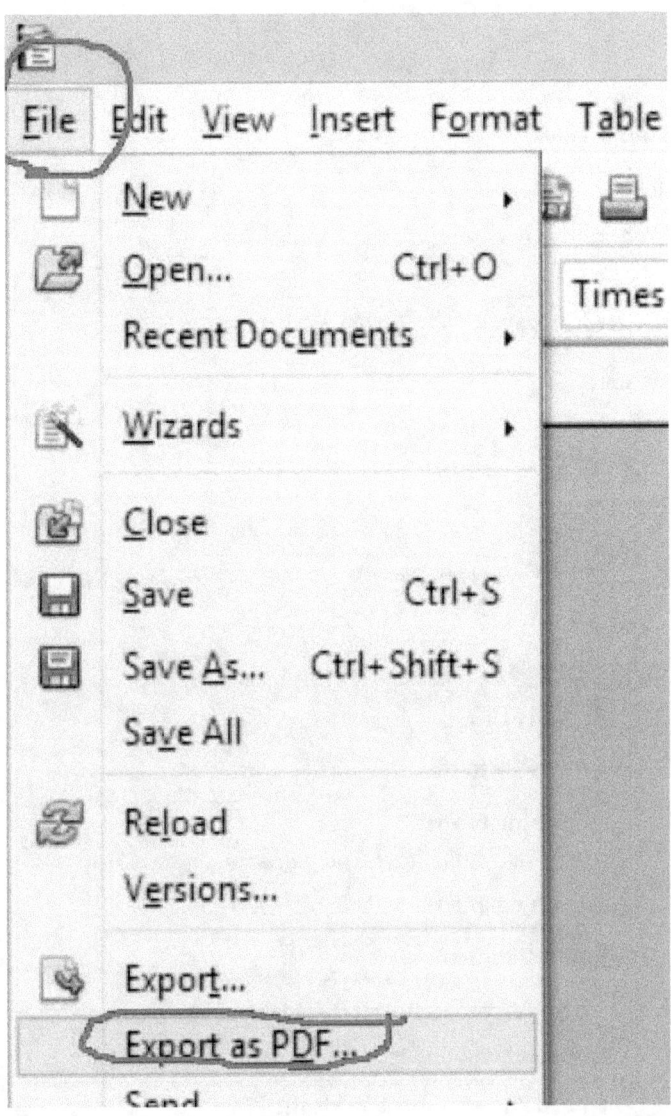

More options! Pay close attention to this next image and choose these exact options.

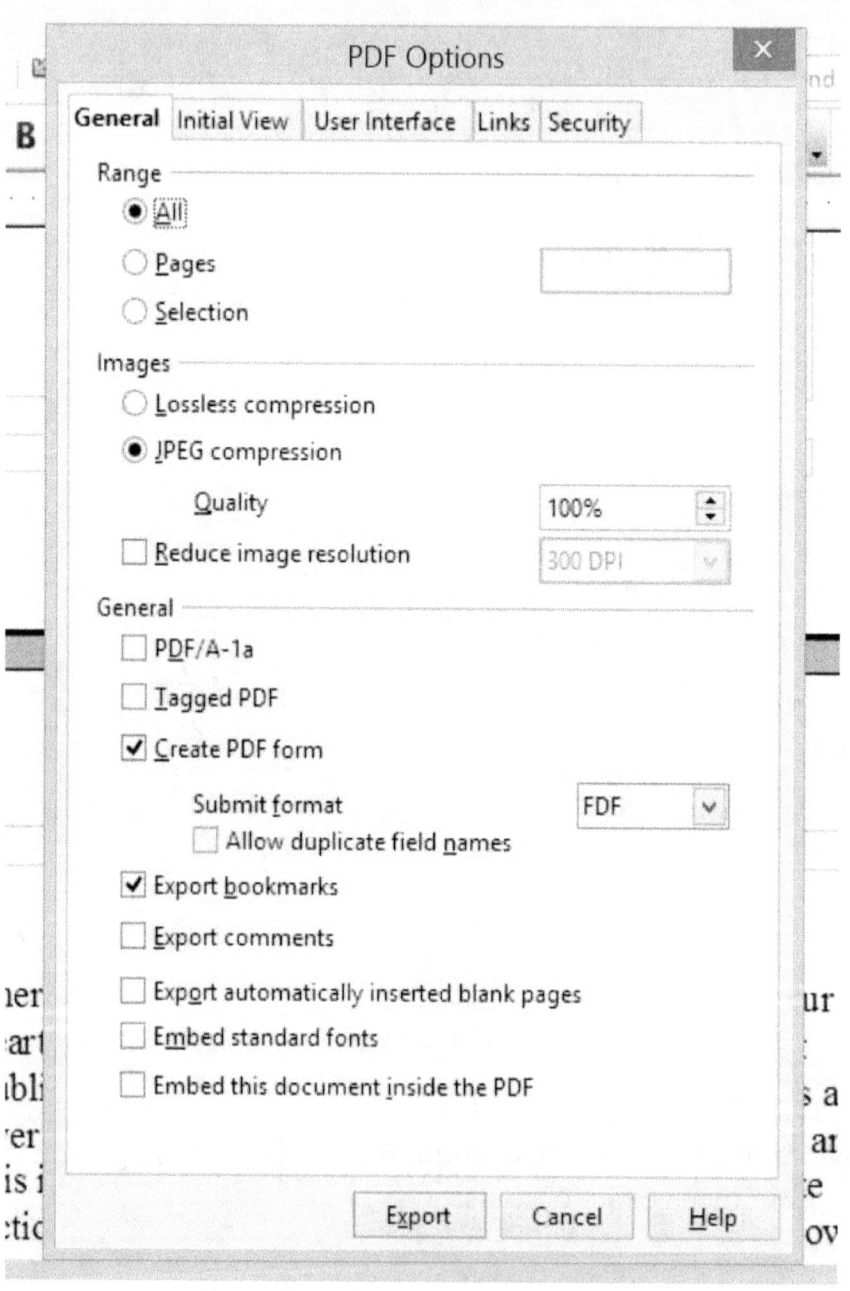

Make sure the RANGE box is checked. Make sure the JPEG COMPRESSION box is checked. Make sure the QUALITY option is maxed out at 100%. Make sure the REDUCE IMAGE RESOLUTION option says 300DPI. This is very important.

Make sure the CREATE PDF-FORM box is checked. Make sure the EXPORT BOOKMARKS option is checked and then click EXPORT. You will be prompted for a location to save the new print ready PDF version of your masterpiece. Put it in the same folder where you have been putting everything else.

The Finishing Touch

Your masterpiece is now in a print ready PDF format. It is time to finish this thing. Log into your Createspace account. If this is your first book, you should see it sitting there all lonely in your Createspace dashboard. Poor lonely masterpiece. Maybe you can create some friends for it later?

Click on the title of your masterpiece and you should be magically transported to your project homepage. This is what mine looks like.

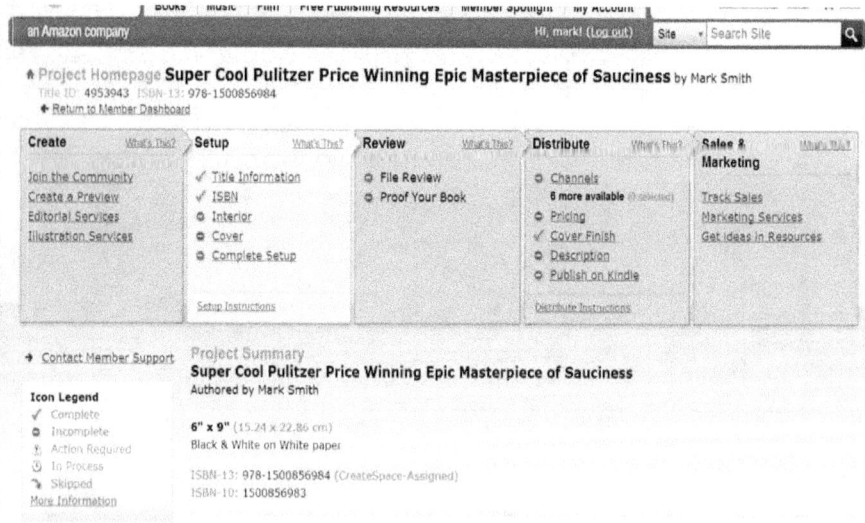

Notice how the SETUP portion is highlighted. Go ahead and click on the word INTERIOR. You should be transported back to the INTERIOR setup section of your masterpiece. Here is what you need to look for.

Choose how you'd like to submit your

Upload your Book File

You can upload your work as a print-ready automated print check will run once your up Interior Reviewer tool.

Go ahead and click the little bubble next to UPLOAD YOUR BOOK FILE. You should now see this.

Upload your Book File

You can upload your work as a print-ready .pdf, .doc, .docx, or .rtf. Your page count will be automated print check will run once your upload is complete. You'll be able to see any issue Interior Reviewer tool.

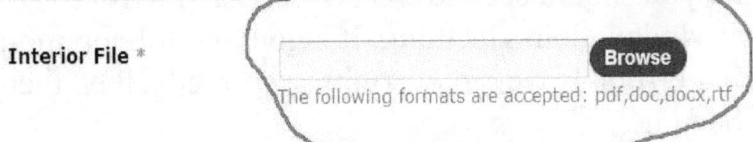

Interior File * | Browse

The following formats are accepted: pdf,doc,docx,rtf

Go ahead and click that big blue BROWSE button and locate the print ready PDF copy of your masterpiece.

Yep, there are more options to choose. You have already formatted your masterpiece for a bleed that ends before the edge of the page. Go ahead and select this option if it is not already selected.

Interior File *

into-the-game-for-print.pdf   **Browse**

The following formats are accepted: pdf,doc,docx,r

Bleed *
What's this?

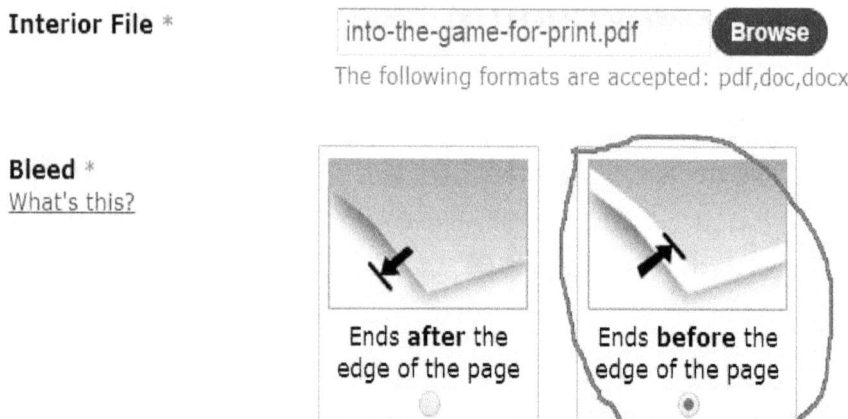

Ends **after** the edge of the page

Ends **before** the edge of the page

Make sure you have the Run automated print checks and view formatting issues online option checked and then click the big blue SAVE button in the lower right corner. The interior of your book should now be uploading! YES!

After that you should see the AUTOMATED PRINT CHECK window doing its thing. It is looking for common formatting errors. If we did everything correctly, then there should be none.
If your masterpiece is image heavy, you may get some warnings about your images not being 300 DPI. Unless you are printing a full color children's book, don't worry about this warning. Your images will look just fine.

If by chance there is some sort of formatting error, Createspace will let you know and provide you with an option to LAUNCH INTERIOR REVIEW. This should not happen if you have done everything correctly in this book. Launch the interior review and see what it says is incorrect and fix it.

Createspace Cover Options

Once you are finished with the Interior of your masterpiece and everything checks out, it is time to work on the cover. The first choice is the book cover finish. You can choose from Matte or Glossy. I prefer glossy. It just looks nice and shiny.

From there, Createspace will want a print ready version of your cover. Createspace does provide a free handy online cover creation tool. I have never used this option. You can play around with it and see what you get.

The second option is to use their Professional Cover Design service at $399 per cover. OUCH! No thanks. You can get a great print ready cover created on Fiverr for $5.00.

The third option is to upload your own PRINT READY PDF cover. This is how I have always done this. I told you I am a control freak when it comes to this sort of thing.

At this point in the game, I know how to make my own covers using a variety of great tools. If you are pretty good at Photoshop, then there is nothing stopping you from making a cover yourself. Go for it. Unleash your inner graphic artist and make a masterpiece!

I am currently writing yet another book on how to create a

perfect book cover. If you sign up to my mailing list, you will be the first to know when it is available and I will offer it free to all my subscribers. Sign up below.

http://eepurl.com/09Pq1

Since creating a perfect cover for your self published masterpiece is way beyond the scope of this book, I will tell you the next best thing. I think you already know what it is. You will need to head over to Fiverr and have someone create a cover for you.

Before you do this, it will help immensely if you can supply them with the proper format and dimensions for this purpose. Createspace has a handy tool for just this purpose and they make it difficult to find. I think they want you to use their cover creation services at $399 a pop. Who can blame them? That's just smart business.

Createspace Cover Dimensions and Properties

Hopefully you are still logged into your Createspace account and you are still in cover limbo. If you are, then look over to the left. Here is what you are looking for.

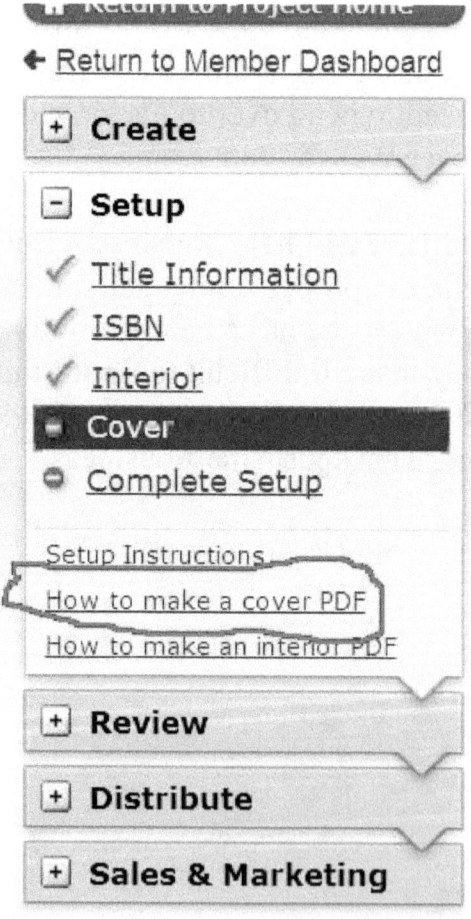

Click HOW TO MAKE A COVER PDF. This will open a new window in your browser with a whole bunch of complicated stuff explaining exactly how to create a print ready cover.

If you are creating the cover yourself in Photoshop or Illustrator, then pay close attention to all of this information. It will help you immensely. If you are going the Fiverr route, then you only need to find one thing: The DOWNLOAD COVER TEMPLATES link.

It should be somewhere towards the bottom of the page right above step 3. It looks like this.

Get a head start with one of our
Our templates make it easier for you to
software that will allow you to open a .png
layout, and bleed for the trim size and pa

→ **Download Cover Templates**

❸ **Design your cover**

Safe Zone

Go ahead and click this link. You will now be asked to configure your template. This is the easiest part. Make the appropriate choices and click BUILD TEMPLATE. All of your choices should look exactly like the image below except for one, the page count. I have no idea how many pages are in your masterpiece. If I happened to guess it correctly, then my psychic powers are working well today.

Configure your Template

Interior Type	Black and White ▾
Trim Size	6" x 9" ▾
Number of Pages	145 pages
Paper Color	White ▾

Build Template

You will now be prompted to download some files. Do it! These are the files you must hand over to your designer. Tell your designer you need the cover as a PRESS QUALITY 300 DPI PDF file. If they are a real designer, they should have no problems doing this for you.

If you are tackling this epic mountain on your own, then

these are the files you will need to create your print ready PDF cover for your masterpiece.

Now the hard part is waiting for that print ready masterpiece to arrive. Once you have your awesome new cover and everything looks perfect, upload it to Createspace and click save. You should know how to do this part by now.

Once the cover has been uploaded, it is time to go over everything once more. DON'T CLICK THE SUBMIT FILES FOR REVIEW button. We're not ready for that yet. We need to setup the synopsis, categories, keywords and other stuff.

Synopsis for Print

Your screen should look something like this.

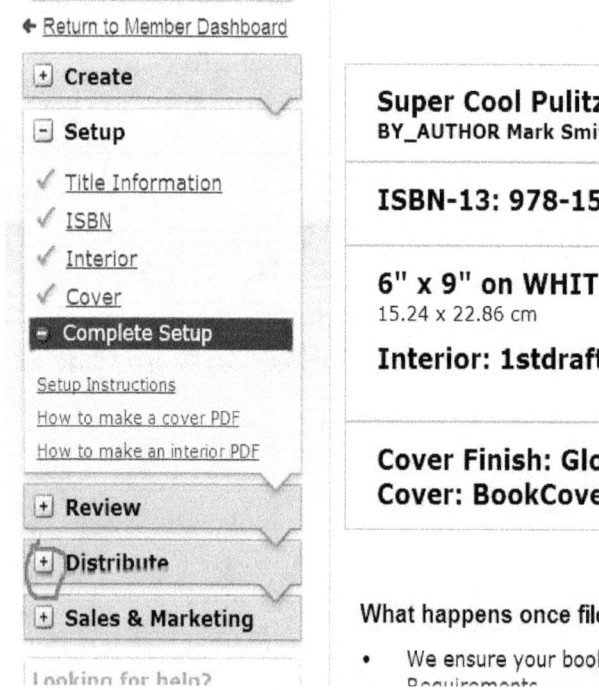

Notice the little tiny plus symbol next to the word DISTRIBUTE? Go ahead and click it. The DISTRIBUTE panel should magically expand. Click the word DESCRIPTION and be magically transferred to the description page.

In the DESCRIPTION field go ahead and enter the synopsis that you worked so hard to create. You can use limited HTML here as well.

Choose the category that best fits your masterpiece. Again, this part can be a little tricky. Do your best to locate the most appropriate category. If your masterpiece happens to fall under the Juvenile fiction or non-fiction categories, you will need to choose an appropriate reading level as well.

Fill out all the other pertinent information like: Book language, Country of Publication, Search Keywords.

The last two options are considered "special" options. Only check the Contains Adult Content if your book really does Contain Adult Content. Don't select the Large Print option either. This is only for books with a font size over 16. You can reformat your book later and choose this to repurpose your content.

Click save and continue. The automated process might throw you to a Publish on Kindle section. Ignore this and click the word CHANNELS in the left DISTRIBUTE menu.

Setting Up Distribution With Createspace

You should be magically transported to the channel selection menu.

The first three options are listed as Standard Distribution. They are Amazon.com, Amazon Europe* and CreateSpace eStore. If they are not selected, then select each one. You do want your masterpiece to show up everywhere don't you?

The next distribution section is called Expanded Distribution. This is how you can get the print version of your masterpiece in stores and libraries all over the world. Sounds like a great plan right? Well it is, but there is one hang up with this distribution.

In order to get your masterpiece into these locations, you will have to offer it at wholesale prices. By the time your book does sell through these channels, you will get very little in terms of a royalty payment per sale. It all depends on how you setup your pricing which we will go over in the next section. Createspace will tell you exactly how much you can expect to get from each book through all distribution channels when we setup pricing.

Getting a lower royalty for each book sale doesn't sound like a great idea does it? The expanded distribution seems to make up for this smaller royalty in volume. It is not uncommon to see orders placed through expanded distribution in excess of 100 books.

I look at it this way. If a reader happens to find my masterpiece in a bookstore or a library which got there through the expanded distribution channels and they purchase it, I have just gained a new reader. That is as long as they don't think my masterpiece is complete trash.

A satisfied reader will happily buy all of your other books. They may look them up on Amazon and buy them for the full retail price where you net a higher royalty. I always enroll all of my books in Expanded Distribution. We are going for total world domination here one eager reader at a time. Expanded distribution helps with the process.

Once you have selected all Expanded Distribution options, click SAVE AND CONTINUE.

Setting Up Pricing Through Createspace

This just might be the single most important part of this entire process. You need to choose a price for the print version of your masterpiece. I suggest you look at the competition and see what they are charging. You may have to undercut them to build up a following. Once the five star reviews start to roll in, you can always raise your price.

Input a price and click calculate. For this example, I chose a price point of $7.99. When you click calculate, you will see how much money you can expect from each sale in each location. I also checked the box labeled: Yes, suggest a GBP price based on U.S. Price.

I also checked the box labeled: Yes, suggest a EUR price based on U.S. Price. You should also note how much your royalties are going to be in British Pounds and Euros.

Setting Up Pricing Through Createspace

List Price			Channel	Royalty
$ 7.99	USD*	Calculate	Amazon.com	$2.64
Minimum list price for this title is **$5.38**		What's this?	CreateSpace eStore	$4.24
			Expanded Distribution	$1.04
☐ Yes, suggest a GBP price based on U.S. price		What's this?		
£ 4.77	GBP**	Calculate	Amazon Europe For books printed in Great Britain	£1.08
Minimum list price for this title is **£2.97**				
☐ Yes, suggest a EUR price based on U.S. price		What's this?		
€ 5.97	EUR**	Calculate	Amazon Europe For books printed in continental Europe	€1.69
Minimum list price for this title is **€3.30**				

These numbers may seem low. Here is a quick way to convert those mysterious numbers to American dollars if that is what you are looking for.

Open up your web browser, go to www.google.com and type Pounds to Dollars. Google is nice enough to display a handy little conversion tool. You can do the same thing for Euros.

If the automatic Createspace pricing adjustment doesn't seem like enough money for you, then change it. It's your masterpiece. It's your destiny. This is all part of the creative freedom you can only get from the self publishing world.

Once you are happy with all the pricing options, click the big blue SAVE & CONTINUE button. When you do this, Createspace will take you back to some choices you have already made.

On the menu to the left, you should see something like this.

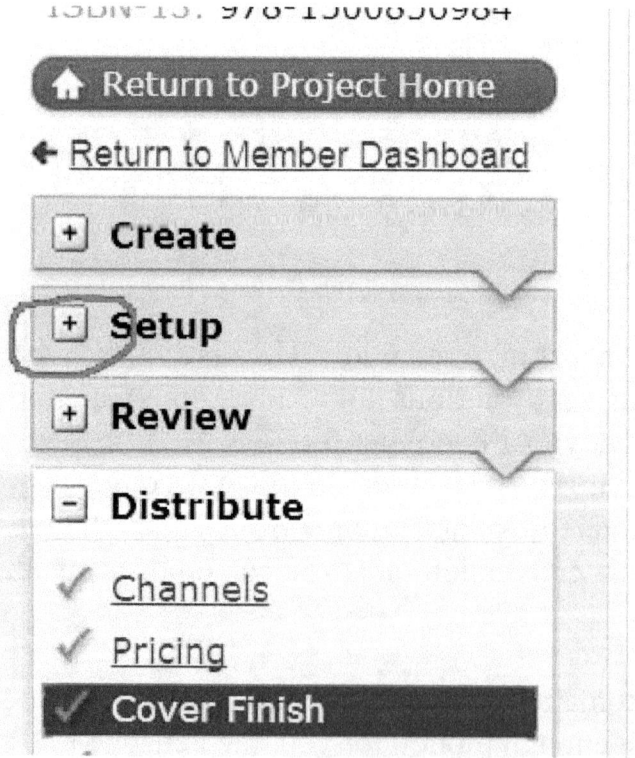

If there are any mistakes with the cover, interior, synopsis, categories or keywords you can fix them later. You CAN'T change the TITLE, ISBN # or TRIM SIZE at this point.

See the tiny little PLUS symbol next to the word SETUP? Go ahead and click it. The SETUP menu should expand. When it does, click COMPLETE SETUP. Scroll down to the bottom right and click SUBMIT FILES FOR REVIEW.

The Createspace team will be hard at work looking over your masterpiece. If there are any problems, they will inform you usually within 24 hours. If you did everything correctly, there should be no problems.

Proofing Your Print Masterpiece

This is the moment you have been waiting for. If there were no problems with your masterpiece, you should now be in the proof stage. This is the exciting part.

Createspace gives you two options for proofing your masterpiece. You can view a digital online version to make sure everything looks perfect, or you can order a physical copy. There is nothing quite like holding that first physical copy in your hands. You worked hard to get to this point and you should be very proud of your masterpiece. If holding a print copy in your hand does not plaster a gigantic smile on your face and put a warm fuzzy feeling in your heart, then you are not human. So which proof option should you choose?

Here is what I do. I choose the digital proof because it allows me to instantly view my masterpiece. It also allows me to get my book to all of the distribution channels much quicker. If you order a print proof, it can take as long as a week to get in your hands.

Look over your digital proof very closely. Break out the magnifying glass if you have to. Have someone else look at it and when you are finally satisfied, approve that masterpiece you have worked so hard on. Createspace will then tell you your masterpiece should be for sale within 48 hours. It is usually much quicker.

Now you can order a print copy for yourself. When it shows up, marvel at your creation. Go out and show everyone your brand new literary child, and then look it over for any mistakes.

You have the ability to change the cover and the interior of your book at any time. In fact, many successful authors will change their covers every six months or so. People become familiar with a cover. Changing it can help spur new sales.

Congratulations! You have done it, but wait there are a few little details you need to attend to.

Linking Digital and Print Editions

Amazon generally does a really good job of automating this process, but not always. The idea here is simple. You don't want your masterpiece to look like two different books. You want both the digital version and the print version to reside on the same exact page at Amazon. This way they share reviews and one version can help inspire more sales for another. It is not uncommon for people to purchase a print version of your book and then purchase a digital version as a companion.

If after a weeks time, your digital and print masterpiece have not been linked, you must contact Amazon and tell them to link your books. To do this, you must log into your Kindle Direct Publishing account. Once you are logged in, follow this link:

https://kdp.amazon.com/contact-us?
subtopicId=linking&topicId=productPage

Fill out the form on that page with all the relevant information and click SEND MESSAGE. You will get a notification from someone at the Kindle Direct team that your books are now linked.

Backing Up Everything

Having a good backup plan is a good idea for anything in life, especially the self publishing world. You have obviously worked your butt off to get this far. It only takes one simple computer crash for you to lose all of your hard work. I am a little paranoid about this and therefore I backup all of my content regularly in the cloud. Oh wait a minute. I forgot to backup the cover I was working on for this book. Be right back.

I hope you took advantage of my free proofreader. If you did, then you are pretty much ready to backup all of your work in the cloud because you should have a Google Drive account. Open your web browser and go to: drive.google.com

Click the big red CREATE button and choose the FOLDER option. Create a special folder just for your masterpiece. Once you have done that, click the big red arrow right next to the word CREATE. This is the upload button. Select all the files associated with your masterpiece and send them to the cloud.

Here is one really cool benefit to storing your masterpiece files in the cloud. You can access these files from anywhere as long as you have an Internet connection. Suppose you have become a moderately successful author. You are enjoying some free time sitting in the hot tub at some posh mountain resort. It's good for inspiration, ya know.

While you are sipping your favorite drink, an idea emerges in your head. It is the best page turning plot twist in the world and it fits perfectly into that new masterpiece you have been working so hard to finish, but your new masterpiece is still on a computer you left at home.

If you have a laptop and you backed up your new masterpiece in the cloud, then you could access it while you sat in the hot tub. Scratch that idea. GET OUT of the hot tub and open your laptop, grab the file from the cloud and type away! Isn't technology great!

Thanks

A big hats off to you for purchasing this book or stealing it from some free hacked site on the Interwebz. Either way, I am sure you learned something you didn't already know about the self publishing world. If you enjoyed the book, please leave a review. I would greatly appreciate it.

Click here to leave a review!

I mentioned several times in this book that I am in the process of creating more books to help you in the often misguided world of self publishing. If you want to be the first to know about them and get a FREE copy, then you must sign up to my mailing list. I promise not to send you email unless it is related to my books on self publishing. Sign up below.

http://eepurl.com/09Pq1

Additional Resources

It would be conceded of me to suggest that my books are the only ones you should read. If you are serious about self publishing, and I would say you are if you have made it this far in my book, then you should read as many books on the subject as possible. The self publishing world is in a constant state of change. There is always something else to learn.

You could start by browsing this book category on Amazon. This list of books will be constantly changing as new ones arrive on the market.

http://www.amazon.com/gp/bestsellers/digital-text/158234011/ref=pd_zg_hrsr_kstore_2_5_last

I would also suggest becoming a member at some of the more popular self publishing forums on the Internet. You don't have to participate in any of the conversations there. All you need to do is browse and consume as much information as possible.

Amazon offers a forum for Kindle authors at the following link:

https://kdp.amazon.com/community/index.jspa?ref_=kdp_REP_TN_cm

Createspace also offers a forum for writers. You can find it here:

https://www.createspace.com/pub/member.dashboard.do

Writing and publishing your first masterpiece is just the beginning. Learn as much as you can on the subject and watch your books sales grow! Now go get busy writing or reading!

www.ingramcontent.com/pod-product-compliance
Lightning Source LLC
Chambersburg PA
CBHW051531170526
45165CB00002B/696